Slave Ghost Stories

Slave Ghost Stories

Tales of Hags, Hants, Ghosts, & Diamondback Rattlers

COMPILED AND EDITED BY

NANCY RHYNE

SANDLAPPER PUBLISHING CO., INC.
Orangeburg, South Carolina 29115

First Edition

Published by Sandlapper Publishing Co., Inc.
    Orangeburg, South Carolina 29115

Manufactured in the United States of America

Cover images from a photograph courtesy of the Library of Congress

Library of Congress Cataloging-in-Publication Data

Slave ghost stories : tales of hags, hants, ghosts & diamondback rattlers /
edited by Nancy Rhyne.
        p. cm.
    ISBN 0-87844-164-6 (pb)
    ISBN 0-87844-166-2 (hc)
    1. Ghosts—Southern states. 2. Slaves—Southern states—Interviews. 3.
African-Americans—Southern states—Interviews. 4. Slavery—Southern
states—History—19th century. 5. Plantation life—Southern states History—
19th century. 6. Oral history. I. Rhyne, Nancy, 1926-

BF1472.U6 S57 2002
133.1'089'96073075—dc21

                                                            2002026858

PROLOGUE

Hags, hants, Jack-o'-Lanterns, boodaddies, plat-eyes, ghosts, and other creatures of the night are the raw materials of Carolina and Georgia folklore. Disembodied spirits, persons who slip from their skin at night, ghosts that ride you, creatures that evolve from one into another at will, and other phantoms have been painstakingly described by cadres of former slaves who lived on Carolina and Georgia plantations. Just when we feel safest, the moon waxes and wanes, mist rolls in from the sea, clouds gather on the mountains, and the air is alive with scary creatures. This has been the tradition for centuries.

Many of the beliefs in supernatural beings arrived with the Africans who landed at Charleston and were dispersed to Carolina and Georgia plantations. The rich folklore that makes the South a special place began deep in the hoard of African cosmology.

As time passed, enslaved Africans held fast to their beliefs and traditions. The many references to

God and "Jedus" in the WPA narratives, however, indicate that numbers of them accepted Christianity. But there was some agreement that the belief in hants, hags, plat-eye, and other hostile creatures that walked the woodlands at night was in line with the character of their new religion.

Some of the spooky creatures, it was believed, were the spirits of the dead who returned to exact vengeance on the living. Hags were defined as real people who learned that trade. Plat-eye took the shapes of various creatures to lure its victims into peril. There were many slaves who never accepted the belief in any non-Christian being, although some of them felt nothing was impossible in the supernatural world. The heirs to the sheen of a far-reaching ancestry imbued themselves with the life and spirit of their time.

The stories of former slaves began to be recorded during the Great Depression. In 1935, when a quarter of the American work force was unemployed, Congress appropriated funds for the Works Progress Administration. President Franklin D. Roosevelt, with the aid of his best friend, Harry Hopkins, issued a manifesto that would provide work for the needy. Among the 3.3 million people employed in the WPA were field workers of the Federal Writer's Project who were instructed to interview former slaves.

By the time the project ended in 1938, thousands of interviews, representing about two percent of American blacks born into slavery, had been edited and transcribed. The collection is on file at the Library of Congress in Washington, D. C., and in select libraries in some states.

Interviewers were not given carte blanche in gathering information but were provided with specific direction. A sample interview with former slaves included, for example, these questions:

- What is your name?
- What are the names of your parents?
- Where were they born?
- Where were you born and how old are you?
- What are your earliest recollections of your pa?

One of the more interesting questions on the list was "Do you believe in spirits?" That question resulted in dozens of stories of hags, hants, ghosts, and other frightful luminaries. It is my belief that the most convincing and entertaining accounts of the supernatural are contained in the WPA narratives of former slaves of the southeastern United States.

My research was done at the Library of Congress, the Caroliniana Library at the University of South Carolina in Columbia, the Wilson and Davis Libraries at the University of North Carolina at Chapel Hill, and Chapin Memorial Library in Myrtle Beach, South Carolina.

The narratives are not presented verbatim. I edited much of the language to make it more accessible. I added bits of information to some accounts to enhance the reader's knowledge of the time, place, and people. More than one WPA narrative was recorded about certain places, giving us additional points of view about the people and the plantation. I occasionally referred to the work of others to make the stories more appropriate and give them extra educational value. As an example, I referred to Dr. Charles Joyner's scholarly books *Down by the Riverside: A South Carolina Slave Community* (Urbana and Chicago: University of Illinois Press, 1984) and *Remember Me: Slave Life in Coastal*

Georgia (Atlanta: Georgia Humanities Council, Georgia History and Culture Series, 1989) in order to check names of narratives voices and place the voices on plantations.

Stories of *beings* outside what is explainable by natural law are found all across South Carolina, North Carolina, and Georgia, but the greatest variety is reported from the Low Country. The Low Country is the tidal area where wide swamps separate habitations and where barrier islands rested for centuries in near isolation. It was only in the last one hundred years that highways, bridges, and schools penetrated community life in many of these sections.

In order that the reader may be able to tell what sort of being each story is about, this book begins with bits of dialogue of people who encountered and described varieties of supernatural beings. Even today, these phantoms inveigle unwary travelers, and many strange forms are spotted along narrow, sandy roads.

Nancy Rhyne
Myrtle Beach, South Carolina

ACKNOWLEDGMENTS

Many thanks to Patrick Kerwin of the manuscript division of the Library of Congress, Washington, D. C., for helping me locate two narratives for which I had been searching. And to Karen at the Franklin D. Roosevelt Library in Hyde Park, New York, for explaining my rights in using information from the WPA program. Lee Oates at Chapin Memorial Library, Myrtle Beach, South Carolina, confirmed the phenomenon of November 13, 1833, to be the most brilliant meteoric shower that ever took place.

There is no way to adequately thank all the librarians who helped me, but I will forever be amazed at the time they dedicated to assisting me in obtaining valuable information for this book. The entire staff of Chapin Memorial Library in Myrtle Beach got involved. I single out Mary Owens for the days she spent arranging an interlibrary loan of the WPA narratives from the Davis Library at Chapel Hill. A lot of the credit for material included in this book goes to the Microfilm Department of the Davis Library. Gary Harris, genealogy assistant at Lancaster County Public Library, Lancaster, South Carolina, assisted with information about the witch trial in that city.

Karen Snell, of the Historical Society Museum on Jekyll Island, helped me with the current status of the ghosts at the house where the duBignon family lived on that island.

Those who deserve the most gratitude and praise are the WPA interviewers. Genevieve Willcox Chandler of Murrells Inlet, South Carolina, introduced me to the slave narratives and the collection on file at the Library of Congress. When I first visited that library, I had only to mention Chandler's name and the whole collection was delivered to my table. The narratives Genevieve Chandler recorded came alive, and they were instrumental in beginning my writing career. The importance of the work of the WPA interviewers is beyond description. It has been more valuable to writers than many people realize.

All of my books are the result of a team effort. Without the help of my husband, Sid, I could not have written them. Once again I owe him a deep debt of gratitude. Without the guidance of Amanda Gallman and her staff at Sandlapper Publishing, my manuscripts surely would have fallen by the wayside. Barbara Stone, of Sandlapper, infused me with her usual gusto. Emerson said nothing great was ever achieved without enthusiasm. This book may not be great, but I would have been on thin ice without Barbara's good cheer.

OTHER BOOKS BY NANCY RHYNE

Slave Ghost Stories

Hags

Plat-Eyes

Jack-o'-Lantern Ghosts

Raw Head and Bloody Bones

Hants

Boodaddies

Witches

Drolls

Ghosts

HAGS

Oh, I have all sorta sperience with hag. They is real people who slip out their skin at midnight and go 'bout tormenting people they know. Hags ride their victim like a horse and suck blood from the neck. The first time a hag ride me, I been a young gal. When men come 'round to court me, gal chillun follow. One of them gal chillun ain't like it 'cause certain boy love me very much, and she set hag on my track. That hag ride me for thirty-three night. My nerves was so work down I fall 'way to skin and bone.

> Maulsey Stoney
> Edisto Island, South Carolina

Hags are able to slip through the smallest crack of your home, while you sleep. On your back, they pummel you to exhaustion, then suck your blood.

> Caroline Johnston
> Colleton County, South Carolina
> Interviewer

Hags know how to shift their skin. That their trade. Hags is real people. They just learn the trade of slipping out of their skin and jump on you and suck your blood. They know how to get back into their skin. A man leave his skin in the loft. He know how to get back in his skin. That his trade.

Matthew Grant
Pawleys Island, South Carolina

Lot of nights I kin feel them riding me. Just the other day I was sitting in a chair and doze off to sleep. All at once a hag jump on me and start riding me.

Henry Bates
Frogtown, Georgia

PLAT-EYE

Plat-eye? They say plat-eye take the shape of all
kind of critter—dog, cat, hog, mule, varmint—and
I hear tell of plat-eye taking shape of 'gator.

Addie
Murrells Inlet, South Carolina

Plat-eye turn to dog, turn to horse, turn back to
people. Turn into a li'l bird! The old head tell
me if you try to run from them they trip you
up! Throw you down. See them better on a old
moon than a new moon. Plat-eye stay 'round
graveyard and they cross the road, 'specially a
road where they have carry a dead body 'cross.
When plat-eye show heself to you, you see him!

Matthew Grant
Georgetown County, South Carolina

JACK-O'-LANTERN GHOSTS

You know Germantown? Over there on the other side of the swamp? My grand live over there. Fanny German. I don't go through the swampy place. Course that be the nearest way to go, but Jack-o'-Lantern live in the swampy place. I 'blige to be scare of Jack-o'-Lantern. It light up 'bout last light, but you can't get close. It move 'round this way and that. I don't want to have no dispute with Jack-o'-Lantern.

Will Alston
Hampton Plantation
McClellanville, South Carolina

Natives of coastal South Carolina believe strongly in "money lights" or Jack-o'-Lanterns, which they maintain hover over buried money, especially in the swamps.

Genevieve W. Chandler
Murrells Inlet, South Carolina
WPA Interviewer

The night be full of "sperrits." One night re-
turning to the beach, a Jack-uh-muh-Lantern
sway back and forth over the marsh. The moon
shine right in the Jack-uh-muh-Lantern face. He
go this way and that. Can't get close to him.

Moses
Tybee Island, Georgia

RAW HEAD and BLOODY BONES

The ole folks tell us that Raw Head and
Bloody Bones will get us if we don't finish our
task. Raw Head and Bloody Bones be ghosts. I
don't want no up and down with them.

Sabe Rutledge
Murrells Inlet, South Carolina

HANTS

Hants, haints, and haants is the same thing. Leave them thing 'lone. Sometime call "uneasy spairits." They live in trees and torment you day and night. They look like shadow of a varmint flittin 'hind you, or in front of you. Hants is frequent 'round the time of the new moon.

Preacher Joseph Holmes
Wilkins, South Carolina

BOODADDIES

Boodaddies are spirits of witch doctors and conjure men released from the body of the living at night for dread purposes. They pester the enemies of voodoo practitioners and the enemies of the conjure man's clients. The spell can only be removed by a charm made by another witch doctor who has superior knowledge of the trade.

Chalmers S. Murray
Charleston, South Carolina
WPA Interviewer

WITCHES

Witches are much the same as boodaddies. They are men and women who deal in conjuring. It is said that when it comes to casting strong spells, men witches are superior to women witches. If the men really put their mind to it, their victim had better make his peace with God.

Chalmers S. Murray
Charleston, South Carolina
WPA Interviewer

DROLLS

Drolls are the spirits of young children who died a painful death. They can be heard crying piteously at night in deep swamps and deserted marshland.

Chalmers S. Murray
Charleston, South Carolina
WPA Interviewer

GHOSTS

After death the spirit travels in the form of a ghost that can change itself into any living thing. There are good ghosts and bad ones. The good ghosts are spirits of persons who have gone to heaven. The bad ones are those who go to hell. A ghost haunts the spot where he was killed, or a graveyard. A ghost cannot hurt you unless you run from it; but should you run and fall down, you will die. Salt and sulfur will keep a ghost away. The sulfur on a match head can protect you. A sprinkle of salt on the door step will ward off ghosts.

Florence Epps
Instructor of English
Walterboro High School,
Walterboro, South Carolina

A ghost is the materialized body of one who is
dead. All ghosts leave the graveyard at twelve
midnight and return at first fowl crow. Some
walk ten feet off the ground and cover long dis-
tances in a surprisingly short length of time.
Ghosts are generally thicker at the time of the
new moon. They do not show themselves to everyone—only the privileged few can see them.
Yet there are some who can feel the spirits of
the departed and hear them speak. Ghosts
manifest themselves in a variety of ways.

Chalmers S. Murray
Charleston, South Carolina
WPA Interviewer

The Stories

HIS SWEETHEART
WAS A HAG

I'm Matthew Grant, from Parkersville,
South Carolina, near Pawleys Island, born 1867.

One time there was a boy courting a girl he
liked. He went to see her and they was sitting
around the fire. The girl's ma and pa came in
the room and sat down. Then the brother and
sister came in and sat down.

About eleven o'clock, the girl's pa took a
bottle off the mantel and rubbed some liquid
on his arm, then on his other arm. His clothes
and his skin slipped right off him. Then he flew
up the chimley. The girl's ma went to the mantel, took the bottle and rubbed some liquid on
her arms. Her clothes and skin fell to her feet
and she flew up the chimley—she ascended like
she was on her way to the clouds. The brother
and sister did the same.

"I didn't know you was hags," the boy said
to the girl he was courting. Just then she went
to the mantel. She rubbed some liquid on her
two arms, dropped her clothes and skin, and

disappeared up the chimley. Gone—all of them: girl, sister, brother, mother, pa. The boy was the only one left in the room.

Then, he thought he had to do like the others. He went to the mantel and rubbed the liquid on his arms. His clothes and skin slid right down to his ankles. Next thing he knew, he arrived at the place the girl's pa went. He said, "I didn't know you was hags."

A vexation came between the boy and the old man. They got entangled there, at the place the girl's pa was to hag that night.

First light was about to come. A hag can't get back in his skin if first light catches him. The old lady and girl and all of them knew how to shift back to day skin. Hagging was their trade. The boy learned to fly quick. And they all flew like birds back to the house and down the chimley. The house was cracking.

Finally the boy told the Maussa at the big house about all of it. Maussa killed out that family—all that race of people. Did away with all of them. Put them in a barrel of tar and burned them up.

WPA interviewer: Genevieve Chandler
Murrells Inlet, South Carolina

THE POWERFUL TIN CAN AND RED STRING

I am Maulsey Stoney, of Edisto Island, South Carolina. I am seventy years old.

A slave boy on Seaside Plantation was born and reared with the sound of the surf in his ear. He breathed the heavy salt air of the South Carolina coast. He knew nothing of the world outside Edisto Island.

One day this boy joined up with some plantation gay blades and they made their way to Beaufort, not too far north of the Georgia state line. They came upon a boxing match in a dark hall on the outskirts of the city. Boys swapped blows with the fist till one was declared a winner. When the Edisto boy noticed some money going to the winner of the boxing match, his interest picked up right smart.

The boy presented himself as a boxer and asked to compete in the ring. His fist was strong and sure, and he was selected to fight. His blows went right to the head of his opponent and the Edisto boy was declared a winner.

He took count of his winnings. It was more money than he ever saw in his entire life.

Dizzy with the new-fangled life in Beaufort, he decided not to return home to Seaside Plantation. Never a doubt wavered his mind that he might have chosen the wrong path. Not only was he making money, but he removed himself from the wealthy bachelor, Ephram Mikell Baynard, the master of Seaside Plantation, who gained the reputation of becoming South Carolina's first millinery. In a few weeks, the plantation boy fetched more money than he ever heard tell of, but he was no millinery.

On a hot June night, after the boy established himself as a promising boxer, old death came climbing over the ropes of the ring. The Edisto boy took a hit to the head that laid him flat on the mat, never to rise again. The next day the boy's body was sent home for burial in the plantation graveyard at Seaside Plantation.

Now, we people of the South Carolina sea islands are careful to observe all precedents, regulations, and rituals relating to the burial of the dead. I might have been a young girl, but I had a lot of patience with the unusual ways of my ancestors. I follow in the footsteps of my

predecessors, and it came as no surprise that
the Edisto boy was buried crossways of the
world. A person who dies a violent death is
buried north to south, crossways of the world.
Never buried east to west. Woe to one who
turns his back to this attitude toward our custom. If a victim of an accident or murder is
buried in any direction other than across the
world, the spirit of the dead person will never
be revenged. The family would be ashamed.

No cup or plate or drinking glass was
placed on the boy's burial mound. That gave
me the awfulest feeling. You always put something the dead person used in this life on the
grave to comfort the spirit of the dead deceased.

Despite tradition, the boy's grave was decorated with only a tin can perforated with tiny
holes. The open end of the can was turned
down on the mound. To the can was attached a
red string. When a white man visited the plantation graveyard a few days after the burial, he
asked an old slave woman living nearby for an
explanation.

"It's this way," she said. "He's buried 'cross
the world 'cause he died bad. If you get killed,
you ain't got no time for praying. When the

man who killed the boy dies, and that is sure to follow soon, mind you, the tin can will draw the spirit of the murderer to this spot. I guarantee. The red string will guide the spirit right down into the grave where the boy lies."

In a few days, word came that the boxer who killed the Edisto boy was killed in the ring. The tin can was the beacon that guided that man's spirit to Seaside Plantation, and the red string was the pilot that steered the spirit into the grave. The spirit of the man who killed the Edisto boy is doomed to lie in the burial spot of the Edisto boy, crossways of the world. That spirit will have no peace, lying down there with the remains of the boy he knocked to his death. I tell people I don't mind speaking about the boy's death and about the spirit that resides in the boy's grave, because it ain't nothing to be ashamed of, and it might make everybody more careful.

WPA interviewer: Chalmers S. Murray
Charleston, South Carolina

THE GHOST OF
AARON BURR

I'm Jesse Williams, age of eighty-three. My pappy is named Henry and my mammy is named Maria. They plowed the fields of Marse Adam C. Walker of Chester County. Mammy plowed same as Pappy, and I ran along behind, taking the dirt off the cotton plants where the twister plow turned the clods on them. When that cotton field got white and red with blooms in summer and white again in the fall, I had to shoulder my poke and go to the field and pick that cotton. I remember the first day I picked a hundred pounds. Marse Adam pulled out a big black pocketbook and gave me a shinplaster, and said, "Jesse, every time your basket hoists the beam of the steelyard to one hundred, you get a shinplaster."

I was born with a caul over my eyes. That means I can see ghosts. When the last quarter of the moon comes in the seventh month of the seventh year, I see the most ghosts. Lying out in the moonlight, just before daybreak, I smell, I hear, I feel, and I see ghosts in the shadows.

Aaron Burr made a speech standing on a big rock near the town hall in Chester. That was before I was born. Aaron Burr was a famous man. He was vice president of the United States from 1801 to 1805. He died in 1836. His only girl, Theodosia, married South Carolina governor Joseph Alston. Burr visited our state many times.

One night I was walking near this rock and the figure of a man jumped up on that rock and looked like he was making a speech. He had on a cutaway coat and a top hat and boots. I could see through him, because he was a ghost. Finally he thrust out an arm. He was shooting at something! Then he disappeared.

When I described what I saw, folks told me Aaron Burr shot Alexander Hamilton in a duel in 1804. From that day to this, that rock has been called the Aaron Burr Rock.

Interviewer: W. W. Dixon
Winnsboro, South Carolina

A DIAMONDBACK RATTLER IN BED WITH THE BABY

I'm Phil Towns of Taylor County, Georgia. I was owned by Marse Towns, called Governor Towns by all but his slaves. He was good to his people.

After a man stated openly he wanted to marry a woman, Marse always required the consent of the parents. Weddings were mostly at night, and no pain was spared to make the occasions cherished ones. The girl was given good clothes, and the celebration was attended by visitors from other plantations. The Towns family gave a big to-do, and the day ended in a frolic, with cake and wine.

During the first year of marriage, the couple lived with the bride's mammy, who instructed the bride in household work. Disputes between the couple were not tolerated. At the end of the year, another cabin was added to the quarters of the bride's mammy and the couple began housekeeping.

One day a man made known his intent to marry a girl named Betty, a cook for Missus Towns. Marse and Missus loved Betty, and they gave her a bigger portion of attention than they gave other girls.

The couple got married and lived by all the rules, and after the first year they moved into the log cabin that was added to her mammy's house.

In due time, Betty had a baby. Missus Towns came every day to see the new baby and check on Betty.

One morning, Betty sent word for Missus to come to the cabin. When Missus arrived, Betty was in the bed, holding the cover up to her chin. The baby was under the cover. Betty said sometime during the night a heavy snake crawled on the bed and tried to get under the cover to the baby. Betty said she held the bed clothes tight under her chin. The snake gave up trying to get to the baby and went to sleep on her chest.

Missus was skeptical. "Betty, there are so many snakes around here, some big as tree limbs. Don't try to make me believe you lay in the bed with your little one and a snake stretched over your chest."

"It's true, Missus," Betty cried.

Missus tried to figure out what the intruder could have been. She mentioned a ghost, but Betty said no. Missus asked if animals have souls. Could the trespasser have been a spirit? Betty insisted she and her baby had spent the night with a large snake on the bed.

But Missus was still skeptical. "The snake must have been very little," she said. "I heard tell that small snakes aren't feared by women in the quarters, and some African women actually carry a tiny green snake in their bosoms. Is that true, Betty?"

"Oh, Missus, that was true a long time ago. But when one of the women got bitten on her chest, she threw away the snake and ran clean down the hill."

Missus Towns didn't believe Betty, but she sent for Luke, and instructed him to bring his gun. When Luke arrived, Missus told him to search the cabin and look under everything. Luke searched all around Betty's bed, looked about the entire floor, and reported that no snake was in the cabin. Another man came in. He looked around but saw no snake.

Just then they heard the sound of death coming from the shelf above the bed. The snake was in its coil. Its bells indicated it was ready to strike.

"Diamond-snake," uttered Missus.

Betty pulled the cover over her head.

In a soft, controlled voice, the Missus said, "Quietly lift the bed with Betty and her baby. Carry it to the other side of the room."

That was done in a jiffy.

"Luke, can you kill the snake?"

"Yessum, Missus," he replied. "It's a diamond-snake, all right, and a big one."

"Then SHOOT!"

Luke took careful aim and fired. The huge reptile fell to the floor. Luke kicked it onto the barrel of his gun and carried it outside. Missus Towns remained with Betty.

Betty's fears did not subside, and she spoke of a snake having a mate. What if the mate comes for the baby? Later in the day, Luke came back to the cabin and said that he had cleaned up a woodpile near the house. The diamond-snake's mate was lying in the woodpile. The second snake was killed and thrown in the river, same as the first serpent.

WPA Interviewer: Adella S. Dixon
Reynolds, Georgia

duBIGNON'S GHOST

I go by the name of Julia Rush. I was born 1828 on Saint Simons Island, Georgia. Ma and my three sisters and me were the property of a Frenchman named Colonel Henri duBignon.

Colonel duBignon was a son of Christophe Poulain duBignon. That family owned Saint Simons and Jekyll Islands. The duBignons had big to-do parties. A heap of people who were highfalutin' came to parties at the big house.

Boating was big too, because the duBignons were members of the Aquatic Club of Georgia. Colonel duBignon owned the *Goddess of Liberty*, a white boat with a blue band bearing twenty-four stars. Colonel started boating in Georgia in 1834 when boats raced at Frederica, on St. Simons Island. The *Goddess* was thirty-two feet long and six oars.

People lined the shore to see the regatta on January 16, 1838. The contest was between northern and southern boats. I was ten years old when I witnessed that race. Southern boats included *Devil's Darning Needle,* owned by

Marse Richard Floyd of Camden County. A green-colored vessel called *Lizard* was thought too slippery to race that day.

Colonel duBignon was a mean-spirited marse. The field hands got up at dayclean and worked till torch light was used to see by. The women who had babies took the chillun to the field in a basket, which they balanced on their heads.

Saint Simons didn't beat the country for cruelty. Texas did that. The overseer would stand in the field with a whip. He ordered, "Heads up!" You start to chop. Meals were brought to you in the field. After you ate, he ordered, "Heads up!" You got back to work. Lots of women fell dead over the hoe. When that happened, they lay right where the body dropped till time to knock off. That was Texas! As bad as old Colonel was, we never wanted to go to Texas. We wanted emancipation more than anything except going to heaven.

All hands were given a certain amount of work to do each day and if the work was not completed, a whipping was forthcoming. Breakfast was sent to the hands in the field. At night they cooked their own meals in their cabins.

Food on Marse's plantation was issued daily
from the corn house. Each person was given
enough corn to make a sufficient amount of
bread for the day when ground. Then they also
dug potatoes from Marse's garden. No meat
was issued. It was up to the slaves to catch fish,
oysters, and other seafood for their meat supply.
We were allowed to raise chickens, watermelon,
and vegetables, which we could sell or keep to
eat.

Colonel duBignon saw that his people had
sufficient clothing. In the summer months men
got two cotton shirts, two pair of cotton pants,
and two pair of cotton underwear. Women got
two cotton dresses, two cotton underskirts, and
two pair of cotton underwear. When winter
came, another issue of clothes was handed out.
Shoes, called brogans, were made of heavy red
leather.

There was little illness on the plantation.
About the only medicine we used was castor oil
and turpentine. Some of the slaves went into
the woods and gathered roots and herbs and
made their own tonic.

WPA interviewer: E. F. Driskell
Atlanta, Georgia

NOTE: The remains of a two-story house where the duBignons lived stands on North Riverview Drive on Jekyll Island. Across the road is the duBignon burial ground, where Christophe Poulain duBignon was laid to rest with the live oak tree as his grave marker. Pictures made of the old house show a lantern in the window. The lantern cannot be seen with the naked eye, and it is believed that's because it is carried by the ghost of Christophe Poulain duBignon, who haunts the old house.

RAW HEAD AND BLOODY BONES WILL GET YOU

I'm Mary Colbert, from Athens, Georgia. Marse John owned me.

We slave chillun played a game to this rhyme:

> *Chickimy, chickimy, Craney Crow*
> *I went to the well to wash my toe*
> *When I got back my chicken was gone*
> *What time, Old Witch?*

Then we ran and chased each other.

We got right rowdy when we played. When folks wanted to scare us and make us be quiet, they talked about Raw Head and Bloody Bones. They said Raw Head and Bloody Bones was going to get us. It's a shame how folks do frighten chillun.

Since I was ten years old I heard all about hants and ghosts. I don't believe in them. I been around so many dead people, I learned that the dead can't hurt you. It's the living that make trouble.

When his Africans took sick, Marse always brought in a doctor. An old woman called Aunt Fannie was set aside to nurse the sick. Dr. Joe Carlton was Marse John's doctor. Now, what I'm gonna tell you is no fairy tale. Once I was so sick Marse John called in Dr. Carlton, Dr. Richard M. Smith, Dr. Crawford Long, and Dr. James Long before they found what was wrong with me. I had the rheumatism and I wore out two pair of crutches before I walked good again.

Dr. Crawford Long became a great and famous man. In 1842, I been told, he was the first to use ether as an anesthetic during a minor operation. It is sure true that when I was a child in slavery he doctored me, but he couldn't cure my fear of Raw Head and Bloody Bones.

WPA interviewer: Sadie B. Hornsby
Athens, Georgia

THE HANT IN TOM PRYOR'S HOUSE

I'm Martha Wright of Georgetown County, South Carolina. I'm upwards of seventy years.

Man, yes man! I always believed in hants. A hant was there in Tom Pryor's house all right. Wouldn't give nobody no rest a-tall. Terrible. Came in there and made more noise on that stove than enough. The noise sounded peculious. That hant always came in the kitchen part of the house. He stayed to the stove and cut up all his craziness in there. Didn't come to the big half of the house and talk. Had more rattle-up on that stove. Sounded like he was going to break up the stove. Francis Gadsden and Georgie sat with me more nights than one for company. I was so feared of that hant.

I didn't go around when Tom Pryor died, but they told me there was a time in that house! Tom died a wicked death. They told me they had to tie him to the bed. If I'd have seen how he died, I'd not have stayed in that house.

One night something talked to me in my room from behind my door. I got mad and I said, "Hant, I want you to talk again so as I can hear you." I was between sleep and awake. He talked kinder funny. And I said, "I want you to talk one more time so I can catch the voice." Never had such a thing happened to me in my life.

I went two times to Parkersville and told the root doctor how that hant did me, and he said, "Work your knee." That meant for me to pray.

I went home and commenced to pray. If I'd not had the Lord in me, that hant would have killed me. I got no rest in that day and time. Maybe catch a little nap in daylight. Sit by the fire and nod. Go to bed—couldn't sleep.

WPA interviewer: Genevieve Chandler
Murrells Inlet, South Carolina

THE MAGIC "HAND"

I'm Phil Towns of Taylor County, Georgia, born June 25, 1824. Governor George Towns owned me. Marse's house was mighty fine, a large no-paint structure that housed a family of eighteen. Eighty-eight slaves were housed in the quarters.

Governor was so kind to his slaves, we were known on neighboring farms as "Governor Towns' free people." Marse never separated families and he made sure the houses in the quarters were comfortable, so as to accommodate the number in each family. And the furnishings were more than acceptable.

Two things provoked Marse to anger: being lied to and being taken advantage of. From early on, slave chillun received excellent training. A boy who robbed a bird nest or a girl who frolicked in a boisterous manner was severely reprimanded.

I believe in signs. The screech of an owl is a sign of death. The bellow of a cow after dark is a sign of death. The howl of a dog after dark is a sign of death. The immediate death of a human being is revealed to animals. 'Though people may find some way around the fear of the signs, the death will come along just the same.

Some slaves who didn't want to work escaped to the woods. They smuggled food to their hiding place by night and remained lost in some instances many months. Their superstition caused them to resort to the most ridiculous struggle to hide themselves.

I'll never forget the man who hid in the woods and visited a conjurer to obtain a "hand" for which he paid fifty dollars gold. The "hand" was a hickory stick, which he used whenever he was being chased. That stick warded off all manner of pursuer. There was one difficulty in this procedure. The stick always had to be set up at a fork or crossroad to work. The man sometime must run quite a distance to find such a spot. When the stick was in place, human beings and even bloodhounds lost the trail. The stick was a magic pole. It had supernatural power. With that stick, the man could stay in the woods long as he liked.

WPA interviewer: Adella S. Dixon
Reynolds, Georgia

THE GHOST OF JOHN WORRIED UM SO BAD

I belonged to Jackson May of Nash County, North Carolina, and I go by the name of Jane Arrington. I was born December 18, 1852.

Old Massa owned a lot of slaves. There were eighty on the plantation. He married Missus Becky Wilder. Missus Becky came from the 'joining plantation, where she was born and where I was born.

Slaves lived in log houses with stick and dirt chimleys. We slept on chicken feather beds. We had plenty of cover and feather pillows. The homes were good, warm, comfortable log houses.

I worked on the farm, cutting corn stalks and tending to cattle. Sometime I swept the yards. I never got no money for my work and we didn't have patches of ground to plant gardens. My brothers caught 'possums, 'coons, and such things, and we ate that most of the time.

My grandmother on my mother's side told me lots of stories about haints and how people

ran from them. She told me that old Missus
Penny Williams, before Jackson May bought
my mother and grandmother, treated some of
her slaves mighty bad. She died and her ghost
came back and nearly scared the slaves to
death. Grandmother told all us chullun she saw
the ghost and knew her after she was dead and
came back.

She told me about slaves that had been
killed by their massas coming back to worry the
mean massa who killed um. John May, a slave,
was beat to death by Bill Stone and Oliver
May. Oliver May was Junius May's son. Junius
May was Jackson May's uncle. The ghost of
John May came back and worried both of um.
They could hardly sleep after that. They said
they heard him hollering and groaning 'most all
the time. The white men groaned in their sleep
and told John to go away. They said, "Go away,
John. Please go away." The other slaves were
afraid because the ghost of John worried um so
bad.

John wouldn't go away.

WPA interviewer: T. Pat Matthews
Raleigh, North Carolina—District 2

ADDIE'S PLAT-EYE

I go by the name of Addie.

Let me tell you about one time when I was clamming. The tide came very late in the evening. It was dusky dark when I hit the Parsonage Lane, light dusky dark. I wasn't feared none a-tall.

I passed the cap'n's barn and stable. There he was, a-milking. And I said, "Good evening, Cap'n Bill." And he said, "Good evening."

I passed the graveyard entrance and kept walking. Then leaving the open air, I entered the dark woods.

I brushed weeping moss aside as I traveled the wet mud in my bare feet. My shoes were tied to my girdle string. Then I got close to the foot log of the old cypress tree. He blew down in the big September gale. And I saw Mr. Bull Frog hit the water. *Ker-plunk.* And a cooter came a-sliding off the log at my feet. I looked at that cooter and then there was a cat, a black cat with eyes like balls of fire and his back all arched up and his tail twissing and switching and his hair standing on end. He moved backward and crossed the cypress log. He was big! Big as my little yearling ox. And I talked to him and tried to draw close. And I told him, "I ain't feared of nothing. Ain't no ghost. Ain't no hant. Ain't no plat-eye. Ain't no nothing."

And I tried to sing, "He carries me through many a danger because He first loved me. He guards against hant or plat-eye, because He first loved me." That plat-eye ain't give me back a word. He moved forward and his tail swished and swished same like a big moccasin tail lashing the rushes. And I braced up. My short-handle little clam rake was in my hand, and I sang, "God will take care of me. Walking through many dangers, God will take care of me."

I raised my clam rake and I came right across that critter's head. My rake was buried deep in the log. And I declare to God, he up and pranced right under my feet, them eyes burning holes in me, and his tail a-swishing, like old Sooky's tail when the flies are bad. If that had been a real cat, I'd have pinned him to that log. I struggled with my rake and the log loosened his grip and I prayed, "Give Addie strength, oh, God."

I raised my rake, and down I came straight

through that critter's middle. His stomach balled up same like the little puffer toad-fish. But that critter ain't feel my lick. And I wrestled like Jacob wrestled with the angel. I was strong and had my bloom on me.

Mr. Plat-eye was just as frisky as before he was hit. And I abused him and cursed him, and I said, "You devil, clear my path."

That critter pawed the air and rose up that big bamboo vine. And I turned back. I hit the path, and I didn't tarry.

Just as I gave God praise for delivering me, there was that cat! This time he was big as my middle-size ox, and his eyes were blazing. I lam him and lam him—and that rake handle was wire that had a nail on it. And just as I made my last lam, that critter rose up before my eyes and he was big as cousin Andrew's full-grown ox. Then he vanished up that old box pine.

Nowadays, when I travel the deep woods and the moss is low and Mr. Cooter and Mr. Moccasin crawl, I tote gunpowder and sulfur. And I carry my stick in my hand. And I watch my step.

WPA interviewer: Genevieve Chandler
Murrells Inlet, South Carolina

SPEAKING 'BOUT
HAINTS . . .

I, Henry Bobbitt, was born at Warrenton, in Warren County, North Carolina. I'm eighty-seven years old. My father was named Washington, after General Washington, and my mamma was named Diasia, after a woman in a story. Us and about forty or fifty other slaves belonged to Massa Richard Bobbitt and we worked his four hundred acres of land. I just had one brother, named Clay, after Henry Clay, which shows how Massa Dick voted, and one sister, Delilah, which shows that old Missus read the Bible.

We farmed—tobacco, cotton, corn, wheat, and potatoes. Massa Dick had a whole passel of fine horses. Our Sunday job was to take care of the horses and clean up around the big house. We worked seven days a week, from sunup till sundown six days, and from seven till three or four on Sunday.

We didn't have many tear-downs and prayer meetings and such, 'cause the fuss disturbed old Missus who was kinder sickly. When we did have something, we turned down a big washpot in front of the cabin door. That took up the fuss, and folks in the yard didn't hear the racket.

There was a lot of haints on Massa's plantation. They put spells on people, and I saw tracks where they rode Massa Dick's horses. Every morning the horses' tails were all twissed and knotted up. I know the haints did that 'cause I saw it with my own eyes.

Speaking 'bout haints . . . I saw a whole lot of things, but the worst that ever happened was when a haint's hand hit me on the side of the head. I bet that hand weighed a hundred pounds and it was cold like ice. I couldn't work for seven days and nights, and I never could turn my head to the left after that. No sirree. The haint did that to me.

WPA interviewer: Mary A. Hicks
Raleigh, North Carolina

THE SEA SERPENT

*The WPA Writers Project director wrote
that a sea serpent in South Carolina's folktales
is rare. This was the only one recorded from
the long coastal strip of more than two hundred
miles. There are several points, however, that
connect with traditional stories of the strange
creatures.*

I am Simon McClair, born on Edisto Island in 1853. When I was a young man, I went
forth on a sailing ship to Chinee [China].
Chinee sure is a funny place. I speck I was
there 'most four months, unloading cargo, and
helping load cargo for the return trip. The ship
was built up right in Charleston and we sailed
from Charleston, and now we going back. Everybody is happy 'cause we going home.

Well, as I say, we set sail. We sailed two
months. The sea was smooth, just like Edisto
Island creek. All we boys got along fine. The
cap'n was a good man. He didn't make us
work overly hard. We scrubbed the deck now
and then. We sat down in the shade of the

mast and main sail. We pranked around some and we sang some.

Things were going too good. The Lord don't mean for you to have too easy sailing, no sir. Mankind gets so careless like, when luck stays good. Some of we boys stopped praying. Some of the boys threw down prayer when they picked up cards. They played cassino and seven-up night after night, and Cap'n didn't like that kind of going on. I hate to give myself praise, but I didn't follow them bad boys. I kept right on praying every night. I thanked God for what He did for me and I asked Him to keep the cap'n's head level.

Came the day when we got to the place where the ocean started to curve down toward the Charleston side. The ocean is flat as a pancake most of the way, but it slants down when you come near South Carolinee.

I speck we been about a hundred miles offshore on that particular day. Lord, it was a calm day! Never in my born life had I seen the ocean so quiet. The sail fluttered and we stopped moving. I didn't like the way things looked, and Cap'n didn't like them neither. Watch out when the sea gets glassy. I depend on signs to observe while sailing around the world. Glassy sea is a bad sign.

Yes, we were stopped dead in we tracks. Ain't made an inch in three whole hours. The sky was blazing blue and, God, the sun was hot. I wiped sweat off my forehead and waited. We just waited.

All of a sudden I heard a flutter in the water off the port side. For a minute I thought it was a porpoise playing around, or maybe a shark. But I was wrong, dead wrong. A big head stuck up out of the ocean. What a head! He was patterned after a snake, and he had ugly eyes and scales all over him. No mistake— the thing was a sea serpent as sure as God made the world. Then the body started to rise. It was big around as a hogshead and covered over with grease.

I yelled to cap'n. I say, "Oh, boss man, a sea serpent is off the port side and I think he is coming onboard."

The cap'n answered, "Let him be, boys. If he comes aboard, he comes aboard. It is God's will."

All hands ran to the port side. The vessel listed over with the weight. The boys stood there with mouths wide open and eyes fair to pop out of their heads. The sea serpent grabbed on the hatch hinge and heisted himself up over the side. We boys parted way and let him pass. He crawled slow-like 'cross the deck and left a greasy track where he been, just like lard laying down in the pan.

I was a church-going boy, but I trembled that day, I tell you. The cap'n got his hand on the Bible. Them bad, card-playing boys started to pray. *Too late, boys. God done sent trouble on we.*

The thing kept right on crawling. Oh, Lord! He reached the main mast and started to climb. He went up that mast just like a snake climbing a hickory tree, and he didn't stop till he got to the tiptop. All the time he breathed hard like a wild boar hog and spattered down lard upon the top of we heads. Everybody stood stock still. Nobody moved an eyelash. We were too afraid.

The serpent was upon top the mast as I said. He twissed around and around the mast so tight I heard the wood crack. Then he cast his eye down and looked in my eye. I never looked in a sea serpent's eye before and pray to God I never do again. He looked like he said,

"Who you think you is anyhow? What I care about mankind? I ain't got you for to study."

By and by he started to crawl down. He came slow, afraid he fall maybe. One of the boys took up a tackle block and chunked it at the serpent. The block hit him square on the head but he didn't seem to mind. Just kept on going.

Cap'n yelled out, "You done it now. Ain't I told you to leave that serpent alone? Bad luck follow we now."

Now, the thing was on the deck. Everybody backed up and let him pass. He took his own good time and greased up the boards just like he did before. He got to the edge of the deck and then he crawled over the side. Soon we heard a splash. That sea serpent gone down to he home beneath the ocean.

Two hours passed and a big wind blew up from the East. The sail bellied, and we flew along same as a bird. When night came, the wind got briefer and briefer and the thunder crashed and the lightning split the sky. We took down every bit of canvas then, excusing the jib. It was the worstest storm I ever sperienced.

He blew and he blew. He blew the lifeboat

away and took the cook's cabin off. He stripped all the hair off the cap'n's head. And that ain't all the wind did! He moved the stove from where he been and put him in the hog pen, and he moved the hog and put him in the cap'n's bed. Everything got mixed up, mixed up. The wind took all we clothes off. We was naked as a jaybird.

But thank the Good Master all onboard was safe. When the wind calmed down, we knocked off work for one full hour and fell on we knees and thanked God for His mercy. We promised not to play cards again, and we promised perzackly not to chunk at a sea serpent or any of His creatures.

The next morning we caught sight of Saint Philip's Church steeple, and we raised a great shout. Home once more, thank Jesus. You brought us through—all the way from Chinee to Charleston.

There ain't a living soul that can get me back on the ocean again. No, sir. Not after I looked in the sea serpent's eye.

WPA interviewer: Chalmers S. Murray
Charleston, South Carolina

"GHOST!"

I am Mary. I live near Cheraw, an Indian name meaning "fire town." I know many stories about old Saint David's Church. I call it The Bell Church, because a mysterious ringing of the bell way back yonder caused people to remember the holy place. Course, it didn't seem so holy on one particular night!

The church building was put up on consecrated ground by the Welsh, early settlers along the Pee Dee River, about the time Marse George Washington was president. The Welsh believed Saint David was their very own saint.

Early in the nineteenth century, a bell was purchased for the church. It swung from a large oak tree near the entrance to the churchyard, as the steeple was not built yet. You might think the bell was used to call the church-going people to divine services, but, no, the bell was used to call folks roundabout together in case there was an emergency.

One evening it was particularly quiet. You could hear the breast feather of a turkey hit the

ground. Sudden-like, the silence was shattered
by the clamor of the bell. Dim figures scurried
about in the darkness.

"What's the emergency?" a man called out.

"Don't know," a voice answered back.
"They're calling us. Something sure done happened."

A few adventurous women joined the men
in hurrying toward the church. Here and there,
oil lanterns and burning pine knots cast flicker-
ing light on the throng, sending forth dancing
shadows of arms, legs, and bodies. The crowd
hurried on, and the ringing of the bell became
even more wild and desperate. It seemed that
an unsteady hand on the rope was urging the
folks to speed up.

"For goodness sake," a man said, stumbling
along. "We don't want to be late."

Peals of the bell came now in uneven
bursts, frenzied jerks. *Clang! Clang!* Pause.
Clang! Clang! Clang! Pause.

On reaching the churchyard, the first of the
crowd stopped short. Anxiety rose in the rear as
necks craned for a better view. Some in front
turned back. Something was too fearful to ap-
proach. Everyone looked toward the bell. Sud-
denly eyes fell on a grotesque figure swaying

back and forth on the bell rope, pulling it vigorously.

"Ghost," a shaky voice whispered. Those in front backed up. Those standing in the rear sneaked forward to get a look at the apparition. The awful, white, misshapen figure fell, clutching the rope, ringing the bell—then he was up again.

A snicker came from behind a bush.

"A calf!" someone shouted.

The crowd burst into laughter. Men and women rushed up to rescue the frightened, snowy white calf. The calf had got his hind feet ensnared in the rope, and the more frantic he got, the louder he rang the bell. Cows roamed the fields and woods free, as there was no stock law before emancipation and for some time after.

Everyone made their way home, all talking about the scare they experienced on that dark night. It was a relief when the steeple was completed in 1827 and the bell was removed from the tree and established in the belfry.

Interviewer: F. D. Slaght, Jr.
Chesterfield County, South Carolina

THE HAG HID HER SKIN IN A GOURD

I go by the name of Rachel McCoy. I am seventy-four years old and I live on Beech Island, South Carolina. But I lived a lot of time at a plantation in Augusta, Georgia.

All the slaves in Beech Island and Augusta knew about the woman who had a habit of going out every night. Her husband couldn't guess where she was gone. He didn't know she was a hag. One night he made out like he was asleep and he saw her get up, reach under the bed, and get a gourd. She did the hag dance, shaking her hips till her skin got loose. Then she began to sing. Her husband heard her singing,

> *Over and under*
> *Through thick and thin*
> *Touch nowhere.*

Then her skin slid off. She put it in the gourd and flew out the window.

The man got up and looked in the gourd. Sure enough, there was his wife's skin, all

curled up. He knew then his wife was a hag.
What could he do to stop her from hagging?
Then it came to him. He took salt and pepper
and sprinkled it over the skin.

Before first light, the wife came flying
through the window. Her skin jumped up and
bit her. She sang,

> *Skinny, Skinny,*
> *Don't you know me?*

She fought with the skin. After shaking herself, she got into the skin, but it just slid right off.

Her husband woke up and said, "Old lady,
who that you talking to? You said, 'Over and
under, through thick and thin, touch nowhere.'"

"I never talked thataway," she argued.

"Yes. 'Twas thataway," her husband answered. He hoisted up the side of the bed
cover. "I'm the one what put salt and pepper
on that skin and here it is."

The woman flew out the window. That was
one hag who never came back again.

WPA interviewer: Maude Barragan
Beech Island, South Carolina

THE COOPER RIVER GHOST

I'm Frank McNeal. I used to live in a shack at the edge of the Cooper River, near Charleston.

Early one winter morning I was waked by a peculiar noise in the river. I heard *Splash! Splash! Splash!* It came to me that someone was seining for shrimp—or maybe a sea horse was trying to catch fish. But the sound was more mysterious than a fisherman or sea horse.

I got up and flung the door open. When I looked at the river there stood a woman, dressed in white, with part of her garment spread over the water's surface. That water was smooth as a polished floor or sheet of glass. All of a sudden she took her head off and threw it toward me. In the twinkle of an eye, she was gone.

I closed the door and went back to bed, but I couldn't sleep. I was afraid my chillun might be tormented by the ghost.

That same week my little boy died. He was not sick so far as anybody could say.

People deny the existence of ghosts but I do not. Some folks think it's all superstition and ignorance. I believe in ghosts because I can see them.

WPA interviewer: Augustus Ladson
Charleston County, South Carolina

THE NINE-FOOT-TALL GHOST

I'm Joe Williams, and I was born in 1851 on a plantation near Charleston.

One night, when I was about ten years old, a friend and me slipped away to visit another. We had to cross a ditch that led to a thick cluster of bushes and vines. When we approached the thicket, about five feet from it we were, there appeared in the center of the path a man, at least nine feet tall. He stood about a foot off the ground, straight up like a soldier. This man didn't have a face. My friend grabbed me and we ran and screamed. A sudden strong wind came up and blew us to the ground.

About ten o'clock we were discovered by a group of people passing. Our nerves were shattered. When we told of the tall man we saw, an old lady told us the man with his feet above ground was said to be the tallest man in the world when he was alive. We were not far from a graveyard, she said, and the tall ghost guarded that place because he lost a girl he loved and that was where she was buried.

Some country folk say, after six o'clock in the evening ghosts leave graveyards to go walking during the night. Some are good and some are bad. Sometimes, two together: a good one and a bad one. The tall ghost was a good one.

WPA interviewer: Augustus Ladson
Charleston County, South Carolina

SID SCOTT
WAS A HANT

I'm Ike Thomas, and I hail from Rio, Georgia. I was born in 1842 on the Thomas Plantation near Monticello, in Jasper County. My ma and pa died when I was a baby.

When Missus Thomas was picking out her personal servants, she selected them by the way they wore their hats. If the hat sat back on the head, that person grew up to be high-minded. But if the hat was pulled down over the eyes, that person grew up to be sneaky, and stole. Missus Thomas didn't want no sneaky and stealing person romping with the folks in her house.

My hat must have been on right, because Missus Thomas picked me to be her carriage boy. I slept on a trundle bed pulled out at night and put under Missus's bed in the day. I always ate when Missus ate, but she fed me under the table. She put a piece of meat in a biscuit and handed it down to me. When company sat around the table, Missus warned me not to holler when I was through, so I would gently touch her on the knee.

I liked to work for Missus because I didn't have to go to the fields. The field hands had a hard time. Every seven years the locusts came and there would sure be a short crop that year. There were so many locusts sometime, they shut out the sunlight. They settled on a field and covered it the same as a blanket. The book of Exodus in the Bible describes a locust plague in old-time Egypt. God sent all sorts of curses, and sometime there were worms that ate the cotton and the corn, or bugs came and ate the wheat. We dreaded those outbreaks, but we were not scared of them.

Only one thing I was scared of, and that was Sid Scott.

Sid Scott was a hant. He was mean, and everyone was afraid of him. He was cut in two by the sawmill. After his funeral, anyone who passed his house at night could hear his hant going *rat-a-tat-tat-bang-bang-bang*, like feet running.

One night when I walked home from fiddling at a white folks party, I had to pass Sid Scott's house. Now, cottonseed was kept in half the house, and the other half stood empty. When I drew close, I made a racket and sure enough the noise started. The moon was about an hour up, and I saw these funny white things run out from under the house and scatter. It scared me at first, but then I saw they were sheep. They found a hole in the cottonseed and got in at night to eat. I 'bout had to laugh.

WPA interviewer: Alberta Minor
Monticello, Georgia.

A PLAT-EYE CAME OUT OF THE WOODS

I'm May Ethel Pickett of Murrells Inlet, South Carolina. Us was going home from church. Came first a little white cat, came out of the woods, came out in the road. Us ran. And then us looked back and there was a little white dog! And us ran again. And when us looked back next there was a white hog. And us ran again. Then, when us looked back, there was a white mule! And next it was a red horse, came out of the woods, came in the road.

When us got to Grandpa's house, he said that was a plat-eye.

WPA interviewer: Genevieve W.Chandler
Murrells Inlet, South Carolina

THE NIGHT
THE STARS FELL

I'm Mary Gladdy. My family has been in Georgia many years. My grandmother, Edie Dennis, was born in 1791 in Hancock County, Georgia, between Milledgeville and Sparta. Old Marse Thomas Schlatter owned her. When she was sent to Columbus, she became the property of Judge Hines Holt. He was a distinguished lawyer. Way back then, Columbus was mostly swampland.

Grandmother talked a lot of times about the old days. Two events she told me about stand out in my mind.

She told me about all the fighting between the white folks and Indians. Once, she was visiting at the home of an Indian family when she heard of an uprising against the whites. The Indians didn't mind my grandmother because she was dark too. She said there wasn't nothing to do that day but stay quiet and listen to the cold-blooded plots to do away with white people. She was frightened 'most to death. The Indians said big chief Osceola would fight till the last drop of blood was shed. When she got home, all the talk there was about the Indian war. She felt kind of stuck in the middle.

Osceola was the one—you might remember—what, with some one hundred Seminole warriors, women, and chillun, arrived at Fort Moultrie, in South Carolina. The chief became ill and died there in January 1838. He is buried at that fort.

Grandmother Edie talked again and again about the night the stars fell on Georgia. She said she looked up and saw thousands of glowing stars shoot across the heavens. She thought the world was coming to an end. If she could have weeded out her fear, she said, it would have been a beautiful sight. All the folks asked what supernatural power held the fate of the world in its hand? Every sign pointed to destruction of the earth.

All the folks on Judge Holt's place were called for a prayer meeting that night. Grandmother always said there was more religion in Georgia on November 13, 1833, when the stars fell than ever before or since.

Turns out, that event was the most famous meteor shower ever heard tell about.

THE HAUNTED
UNION CHURCH

My name is Azile, and I'm from Union, South Carolina. I want to tell you about a church hereabouts that is busy with evil spirits.

The choir loft of that church was built over the very spot where two field workers were buried before emancipation. The pipe organ was installed there too. The bodies that were buried under the choir loft and pipe organ were removed before the church was built, but the ghosts of those men stayed right there.

One day each week the organist, Miss Ruff, and her substitute organist went in the church to practice in quiet for the upcoming service. On one occasion, as the music rose 'most to heaven, they heard a loud slashing, sweeping noise, like a well-dried brush broom sweeping a plantation yard. Then came a creaking and moaning what gave an eerie and creepy feeling to the two women.

Right quick, they gathered up their music sheets and jumped over the partition between the choir and pulpit and ran for the nearest door. Neither one went to that church at night to practice again.

Bear with me while I tell you my recollection of one event when I went to clean the church.

It was in the middle of February. Me and Geneva were there. I was out in front and Geneva was behind me. I reached out my hand to dust off the organ when I heard the awfulest noise what ever been heard. Sounded worse than brush brooms! I burst through the door and ran down those steps so fast my hair stood up. Geneva was right on my heels. She was so close I thought the hant had caught up with me! I reached back and swung my broom, and Geneva yelled, "Stop hitting me. You crazy?"

We were out in the yard by then.

We told Jake, the janitor, we weren't going to clean that church no more. We didn't blame Miss Ruff for not going there and playing that organ less lots of folks went with her. That church is haunted and them spirits are acting up—in the daytime at that! Folks done got so wicked the devil is going right up in the church altar after them.

Now, me and Geneva didn't see nothing, 'cause we got religion, and when you got that, the hants don't bother you by letting you see them. But if you ain't got religion, they will surely show themselves.

WPA interviewer: Caldwell Sims
Union, South Carolina

THE HAINTS

They call me Mad Griffin. Yes, sir, Mad is my name, and I'm eighty-two years old.

When I was a boy on the plantation near Whitmire, South Carolina, Marse Glenn had sixty-four slaves. On Saturday night, we darkies had a little fun on the side. A way off from the big house, down in the pasture, there was about the biggest gully I ever saw. That was the place where we collected 'most every Saturday night for our little mite of fun away from the white folks' hearing. Sometime it was so dark you could not see the fingers on your hand when you raised it before your face. Those were the scheech nights. The scheechiest I ever witnessed in all my natural born days.

Then, there were the moonlight nights when you could see. Then you saw too much. The pasture was big and the trees made dark spots in it on the brightest nights. All kinds of varmints hollered at you when you were going along to that gully.

We went in droves sometimes. Sometimes we went alone. When we started together, we

got separated before we reached the gully. One
of us would see something and take to running.
Maybe the others in the drove wouldn't see
nothing just then.

That is exactly how it is with the spirits.
They might show themselves to *you* and not to
me. They act real odd all the way 'round. They
can take a notion to scare the daylights out of
you when you're with a gang, or they scare the
whole gang. On the other hand, they can show
themselves off to just two or three. It ain't never
no knowing as to how and when those things
will come into your path, right before your very
eyes—especially when you're partaking in some
dark secret where you plan to act real quiet all
the way through.

Those spirits were light on dark nights.
They shone themselves just like lanterns. On
moonlight nights, I saw them look at first dark
like a tree shadow, then they got real scary
white. It ain't no use for white folks to allow
there ain't no haints, 'cause I know. The white
folks just don't have eyes to see such as that,
but the haints are there just the same.

We used to steal a hog every Saturday
night and take off to the gully where we had a

barbecue. We dressed and cooked the hog and
had the most fun. Since we had no religion, we
felt no scruples about not getting Marse's meat
ready for Sunday.

We'd get back to the big house along in
the evening on Sunday. Then Marse would
come out in the yard and allow where we
chillun was this morning. We told some lie
about going to a church meeting. But we got
scared and decided the best plan was to do
away with the barbecue in the gully. Conjure
Doc said he put a spell on old Marse so he
would believe everything we told him about Saturday night and Sunday morning. That gave our
minds some relief.

But it turned out, in a few weeks Marse
came out from under that spell. Doc never
knew nothing about it. Marse began counting
his hogs every week. When he caught us, we
were all punished with a hard long task. That
cured me of believing in conjure and charms,
but I still know there are haints. Every time you
go to that gully at night, you hear hogs grunting
in it, but you can't see nothing.

After Marse Glenn died, all the white folks
left the plantation. Some folks, not of the qual-

ity, came to live there and run the plantation.
Wasn't long before they pulled up and left.
They allowed as how the house was drafty and
they couldn't keep the smoke in the chimley
and the doors would not stay shut. They also
allowed that folks prowled around in the yard at
night keeping them awake.

Then Marse Glenn's boys put Mammy in
the house to keep it for them. Mammy said the
first night she stayed there the haints let her get
not narry a mite of sleep. We all allowed that
was the reason the white folks left out so fast.
When Mammy could not live in that big house
where she had stayed for years, it was no use
for nobody else to try. Mammy allowed it was
Marse's spirit looking for his money that he
buried and the boys couldn't find no sign of.

After that, the sons tacked a sign on the
front gate, offering two hundred dollars to any
man, white or black, that would stay there and
find out where that money was buried. Our
preacher, Reverend Wallace, allowed he would
stay there and find out from the spirits. He
knew they were trying to show the spot where
that money was.

He went to bed. A dog ran down the steps.
A black cat ran across the room, then it turned

to white before it ran into the wall. Then a pair of white horses came down the stairway rattling chains for a harness. A woman dressed in white came into that room. Brother Wallace up and lit out of that house and never went back.

Another preacher tried staying there. He said he was going to keep his head covered plumb up. Something uncovered it and he saw a white goat grinning at him. But as he was a brave man and trusted the Lord, he allowed, "What you want with me nohow?" The goat said, "What are you doing here?" The preacher said, "I want you to tell me where old Marse hid that money." The goat grinned and allowed, "How come you don't look under that pillar on the porch?" Then he ran off.

The preacher hopped up and went out on the porch. He removed that pillar the goat said. Sure enough, there was the money. It appears like it was the pillar on the left end of the back porch.

Don't tell me there ain't no haints. I been had too much experience with them.

WPA interviewer: Caldwell Sims
Union, South Carolina—District 4

THE STARS
COMMENCED TO FALL

I'm Phil Towns, and I hail from Taylor County, Georgia. I sprung from my granpappy and granmammy who came from Africa. Granmammy Hannah lived to be 129 years old. I was born June 25, 1824, number four of thirteen chillun. Pappy was a field hand and mammy did light work in the big house. Marse never had no clocks. We worked by the sun.

I recollect the night of November 13, 1833, when all the stars commenced to fall to the earth. The people been struck with astonish. I was nine years old when the stars shot across the heavens, numbering like raindrops in a big storm.

People say, "Why you never keep some of them stars?" That was because I was afraid to touch them. Besides, they were 'most too hot to touch. And they were different from stars. They were black as a no-moon night and they were scattered like seeds. There was a multitude of the dusky critters. I didn't know what they were.

I heard tell the earth passes through the thickest part of the swarm every thirty-three years.

Many people took to their knees that night. Mammy and Pappy thought judgment day had come. It wasn't judgment day and it wasn't emancipation. It was the night the sky fell on Georgia.

WPA interviewer: Adella S. Dixon
Reynolds, Georgia

THE HAG RODE ME FOR THIRTY-THREE NIGHTS

I'm Maulsey Stoney, age of seventy-nine. Living on Edisto Island, it should not surprise that I have many experiences with hags. Some enemy put a hag up to the devilment, I know.

Back yonder, in slavery times, when a young man came around to court, girl chillun followed along. I expects one of them girl chillun didn't like it 'cause a certain boy loved me very much. She set a hag on my track.

Anyhow, the hag came to see me. I remember good when I caught sight of him. I was fixing to go to bed and just as I put my feet upon the step, a green light burst in before my eyes. Then I saw a black, raggedy-looking thing ascend the steps. Blood-red light shone out his eye. I opened my mouth to yell, but my jaw locked. That hag rode me all that night and the next thirty-two nights.

My nerve was so worked up I fell away to skin and bone. I got scarcely a wink of sleep for that long time. When I rose in the morning, I felt like somebody had beat me with a stick. Pain ractified my body. All kinds of things crossed my mind. When I dropped off to sleep, my sleep wasn't natural. I saw crows descend upon my pea patch and carry off every single pea. I saw many things such as that.

Mammy asked me, "What's the trouble?" I didn't answer. Something locked my jaw.

"What ails you, Maulsey?" she said again. "I bet you been playing with bad chillun. You in that very same crowd what robbed buckra's peach trees, if I ain't made a bad mistake."

I had to swallow all those words my mammy proclaimed 'cause I was too scared to speak. Just shows what a hag can do to you when he has a mind to.

Came one day my mammy got worried about my ailment.

Mammy said, "Maulsey, I got a notion a hag been riding you at night. That so? I'm going to find out. I know exactly how to fix a hag, and how to fix him so he stays fixed. Go lie down on your pallet. When you wake up in the morning, you'll feel much better. I guarantee."

Mammy sat in my room beside my bed.

She had a needle in her hand, ready for the hag.

Just as Mammy said, when I waked next morning, the spell had dropped off me and my nerve came back. I felt so good I ate two whole mullet, drenched down with gravy, and almost half a pot of hominy.

Three mornings, hand running, an old lady came to the door and begged for salt. I was extra careful them days. I didn't give one inch. The old lady was the same hag what rode me, sure as God's in His heaven. If I gave her anything, especially salt, I would give her back the hag-body my mammy caught. Course, you know hags can slip out of their skin at night and fly all kinds of different courses. That's the gospel truth.

Next night after I fell asleep upon my pallet, Mammy took her seat alongside my bed and watched. She had her bottle of herb physic close to hand to keep up her nerve. The herb is soaked with whiskey or it don't work on you right. By her feet rested an empty bottle with a cork in its mouth.

Mammy watched and watched, and caught a nap every now and then. Just before first fowl crow, she saw my body stir. The hag was getting ready to ride me. My stomach started to twitch and heave. Mammy was quick. She reached down and got the empty bottle. She uncorked it, then placed it on my stomach with the mouth turned down. All that time her left hand fumbled in her dress for a needle. Ain't no time to lose—a hag is too fast for slow people and gets away.

Mammy found the needle. She was ready for that hag. She counted up to thirty-three and lifted the bottle off my stomach. Then she threw the needle in the bottle quick and corked it up before the hag recollected herself. Got him now. Mammy done got him. That hag ain't going to worry me no more. The hag is clean gone.

And that's how my mammy caught the hag and lifted the spell. She rests in she grave now. Live and learn. Die and forget all.

My mammy waited till I grew up before she explained the whole business. She said a young girl's mind is too weak to stand up to it. My mammy knew about most things.

WPA interviewer: Chalmers S. Murray
Charleston, South Carolina

THE ROAR OF
THE SEA HORSE

Although this is not a slave narrative, it is among the interviews with residents of the South recorded during the Works Progress Administration. Because of the importance of the story—and the rarity of its subject matter in southern folklore—it has been included with this collection.

I'm Polly Maddox of Union, South Carolina.

Sea horses really do live in the Mediterranean and other seas. Those are quite small. They are of the genus Hippocampus, of the pipefish family, having a prehensile tail, an elongated snout, and a head bent at right angles to the body. They swim vertically only. The sea horse in this story was a very singular one. Its length and breadth was of immense size, its voice louder than any other sound on the earth. How the sea horse got into the bottomless horseshoe of the Broad River at Leonard Hall remains a mystery.

The bottomless horseshoe was the most perfect horseshoe bend on the Broad River. It measured one-hundred-sixteen-feet deep. The bottom was quicksand. The water came so swiftly around the horseshoe, it made great inroads into the bank on the Union County side of the river. The lands of Leonard Hall extended down to these banks. My aunt, Miss Edith Murphy, owned Leonard Hall, a boarding house. My grandmother, Mrs. Sallie Murphy, told me the story of the giant seahorse that lived in the river.

This is the story she told me:

"Long, long ago, when I was a child, there was a river town called Reidstown. It was a thriving place on the Green River Road, where stagecoaches stopped with travelers from Charleston and Columbia on their way to North Carolina. Scenery and climate were so delightful many strangers tarried long in the town. It was quiet and peaceful—except when the sea horse roared. The roar was so loud that anyone standing on the surrounding earth could feel the tremors from the vibrations caused by its powerful voice. The Pinckneyville ferryman said his ferryboat was often turned nearly upside down by the waves caused by the sea horse's roar.

"These terrible roars came usually at night, when the countryside was sleeping. Some field hands were so frightened by the monster's roars they ran away from home, going upriver into North Carolina, never to return.

"The sea horse at Leonard Hall had a head like a horse. Like its roar, its body was enormous. It swam vertically, like its smaller relatives, and surfaced only to grab some unwitting prey. Many people, including some Indians, were overcome by its hypnotic influence and fell into the river. When they hit the water, they fell astride the seahorse and rode to the bottom of Broad River, disappearing forever.

"The continuous roaring of the sea horse so jarred the land about Reidstown, people were afraid to build houses there, for fear they would tumble down. Natives were so frightened, they couldn't work. Strangers no longer stayed in the town, and stagecoaches changed their routes to avoid the area. Finally, Reidstown was abandoned. And, not long after, all the river towns along that stretch of the Broad River died out.

"Since the demise of Reidstown, the voice of the sea horse has been silent. The monster has not been sited again in the vicinity of Leonard Hall. But those of us who heard that roar believe he is still there in that Horseshoe Bend waiting for people to return."

WPA interviewer: Caldwell Sims
Union, South Carolina

THE FALLING STARS

I'm Rastus Jones. I was the property of
Massa Sidney Jones, a Chapel Hill, North Carolina, planter. I know I am at least one hundred
years old—though I don't remember exactly
what year I was born.

Massa moved from North Carolina to
DeSoto County, Mississippi, taking all we slave
Africans with him. We made the trip in wagons.
In the two places, North Carolina and Mississippi, it was a customary of Massa to give each
slave an acre or two of land to work for himself
and reap any profit come from it.

Massa was good to his slaves, giving us
clothing each spring and fall. He issued shoes as
needed, fed us well, and furnished medical attention when we were sick. Massa's chillun
played with the slave chillun, same as one. At
Christmas time, we slaves were always remem-
bered by Massa with gifts.

My first memory is the falling stars on November 13, 1833. That establishes my birth, I
reckon, at about 1825. I remember that night
like it was yesterday.

"Wha? Wha' is it?" we chillun asked. You couldn't keep no distance from the stars, 'cause they fell all around, everywhere. Some folks roundabout said it was spirits. People went down on their knees, every muscle in their body acquiver. Called out to God. Asked Him to calm the heavens. But the heavens combusted that night.

It wasn't spirits or ghosts, I came to find, but the most brilliant display of the Leonids I ever heard tell of.

WPA interviewer: Alberta Minor
Georgia WPA District 6

HOW TO BECOME
A WITCH

I am Herndon Bogan, age of seventy-six. I
was born in Union County, South Carolina, on
the plantation of Doctor Bogan, who owned my
mammy, Issia, and my pap, Edwin. There were
six of us chillun: Clara, Lula, Joe, Tux, Mack,
and me. There were a heap of slaves on Doc's
plantation, maybe a hundred and fifty. We
worked hard, but we had plenty to eat and
wear, even if we did wear wood shoes. My pap
was given to the doctor when the doctor was
married.

I saw a heap of cocks fighting in pits and a
heap of horses racing. Marster had lots of thoroughbred horses, and when he won, he gave his
slaves a big dinner and a dance. If he lost, oh!

One day, I heard an old woman slave tell
about witching in Mecklenburg County, North
Carolina. She was around ninety, so I reckon
she knew what she talked about. She said if
anybody wants to be a witch he draws a circle
on the ground, just at the edge of dark, and

gets in the circle and squats down. There he has to sit and talk to the devil and say, "Make me a witch." After that he has to boil a black cat, a bat, and a bunch of herbs and drink the soup. After he's done that, he's a witch.

WPA interviewer: Mary A. Hicks
North Carolina District 2

NELLIE'S HANT HOUSE

I'm Nellie, and I was born with a caul over my face. I see hags and hants and ghosts because I have that gift. Yessir.

So many hags and hants at my house I asked Massa to build us another house. Massa refused. I called my house the "Hant House," but hags were so frequent it could have been known as hag house. Hag came 'most every night, but I did something to hold him back. I needed my rest.

I hoed. I planted. I harvested. Night come, I craved for rest. I didn't get no rest. Come first dark, I bolted the door. I ate my bittle. I bedded down the fire. I fell in my bunk. But I didn't outen my lamp. Kept it burning low to keep hags out. And the flour sifter was hung over the keyhole. When a hag came through the keyhole, he got in that sifter. He has natural curiosity. He stayed right there till he counted the holes in that sifter. He lost count, he started again. And he counted. And he got mixed up. Then daylight caught him. He had to go. Had

to go get back in his skin before first fowl crow.
I know.

I fixed the flour sifter to keep hags out.
Hags can't trouble me. Hags are human. Hags
can't leave a flour sifter alone without counting
the holes, and a hag can't count the holes before first fowl crow. Hags can't manage a flour
sifter.

WPA interviewer: Genevieve Chandler
Murrells Inlet, South Carolina

I FIXED THAT HAG UP
GOOD AND PLENTY

My name is Penny Williams. I was born at the Hinton place, about three miles south of Raleigh, North Carolina. And I am seventy-six years old.

We belonged to Marster Lawrence Hinton. My mammy was Harriet Moore and pappy was Mack Moore. They belonged to Marster Moore first.

Marster Lawrence owned 'round two hundred slaves and about four hundred acres of land. We had enough to eat, such as it was, but that ain't bragging. And we were punished pretty bad if we complained, sassed, or refused to work like we should. Nat Whitaker was the overseer and the patteroller, and he was strict, I'm telling you. I saw him beat slaves till the blood ran.

Some slave men went courting on other plantations in spite of the devil, and the marster hadn't given them no passes. They went courting without passes, and the patteroller's beatings wouldn't stop them. At last Marster Lawrence decided to hang cowbells on their necks so he could hear them if they tried to cross the property line and go courting with a girl who lived on somebody else's plantation. The men couldn't get the cowbells off their necks. They had to court the girls on Marster's plantation.

One night a hag tried her best to ride me. I was in the bed, and she thought I was asleep. That no-skin hag came flying through the window. I felt her when she crawled up on my left leg. It felt like a jellyfish—like jelly or rubber, sticky like. The circulation stopped in that leg. Before the hag got up to my neck to suck the blood, I got up and found a knife and put the knife under my pillow.

From that day to this I sleep with a knife under my pillow. Since that time I ain't had no more trouble with hags, or the circulation in my legs neither. I fixed that hag up good and plenty.

WPA interviewer: Mary A. Hicks
North Carolina District 2

NELLIE'S HANT HOUSE
HAD TO BE MOVED

My name is Zena. I married my sweetheart George before I was seventeen. We lived in Maum Nellie's house 'cause she done moved out. Just like Maum Nellie, I was born with a caul over my face.

One night when the moon was full, I heard a strange noise way 'cross the field. Hant coming through the pecan orchard! The hant is worse at the full of the moon. It barks like a fox, howls like a dog, hoots like a squinch owl, sounds like all the beasts in the woods.

When the hant hit the house, it circled. It prowled same like a stray dog. I kept still so he would think nobody was there. I held my breath, then I saw the door I done bolted move open. That hag moved all 'round the house. The pot lid lifted. The rocking chair rocked. The more I kept still the more that hant prowled. I watched him. He crept 'round.

Next day George said he'd fix the hant. He got his gun. When first dark came, he waited.

He dozed in his chair. Come twelve o'clock the moon been for rise. I heard that critter howl. I said, "Hear that! Hear that!"

George rose up and took notice. That hant prowled. He hooted like a horn owl. He sounded same like a little squinch owl. He barked like a fox. He howled. He cooed like a dove. He bellowed like a 'gator. He made all them noises. And he tried to open the door. When that door cracked, George braced himself and fired both barrels. He 'most tore the house down but he didn't get the hant.

Next night, George's friends came. They all had guns. They sat up and they all fired, but they wasted the powder and shot.

I surely needed me rest. Washing and chopping wood and working all day I got dead tired. But that hant didn't let me eat nor sleep.

Old people said we house had to be taken down. The men took it down plank by plank and moved it 'cross the road. There is them what say if the hant is in the house, the hant stays there. But that's all they knew to do—move the house.

Some said there was murder on the spot where that old house sat. So they dug. And they dug. And down about six feet, they threw out a cedar log what been burned and charred. Under that log was bones. Some said they was critter bones. Some said they weren't. I ain't know. But I tell what I know.

I been born with a caul. I can see what the ordinary, common run can't see.

WPA interviewer: Genevieve Chandler
Murrells Inlet, South Carolina

THE RATTLING CHAIN WAS A HANT

I'm Harriet Miller of Toccoa, Georgia. I was born in 1826. Pappy was a Cherokee Indian name of Green Norris, and Momma was a white woman name of Betsy Richards.

When I was three years old, Momma gave me to Marse George Naves. He lived in the mountains of South Carolina, just 'cross the river. Marse Naves didn't own his home. He was overseer for old man Kennedy Jarretts.

My white folks tried to send me to school, but the other white folks wouldn't receive me in their school on account of I was mixed. There weren't no colored schools nowhere. Miss Sallie Jarrett taught me some.

If slaves stayed in their place, they weren't never whipped or put in chains. When company came, I knew to get outdoors. I don't remember getting but three whippings in my life. Missus had brown sugar in a barrel setting in the dining room. She would go off, and she would come back and ask me 'bout the sugar.

She would get after me 'bout it and I would say I hadn't taken it. And then when she turned my dress back and whipped me, I couldn't hardly sit down. She whipped me twice 'bout the sugar and then she let me alone. T'wasn't the sugar she whipped me about. She was trying to get me to tell the truth. That was the best lesson I ever learned, to tell the truth, like David in the Bible.

When slaves got sick, the white folks looked after them. The medicines was mostly herbs. Boneset was made into tea for colds. Butterfly root and slippery elm bark was used to cool fever. Willow ash was good when your feet hurt.

Did I see Indians? Yes'm. Once, a group camped on the river bottom for three or four years. Me and my friends went down nearly every Saturday to hear them preach. I couldn't understand what they was saying, but we enjoyed it just the same. The Indians didn't make no racket like we Africans. They would sing, and it sounded all right.

The Indians grew crops. Raised ponies, pretty ponies. Made baskets out of cane, the beautifulest baskets, and they colored them with natural dye. Nobody bothered the Indians.

Indian women wore long dresses and beads. Their hair was plaited and hung down their backs. Their babies was tied in a blanket on their momma's backs. Men wore breeches and feathers in their hats, no shirts. You should have seen them cooking. They boiled birds in a big black pot. They made corn dough dumplings and dropped the dumplings in the pot with the birds. Terrible—putting dumplings in the pot with the birds! We never saw such as that.

Indians had blow guns. The guns was made of cane, 'bout eight feet long, and burned out at the joints for the barrel. They used sharp arrows. They slipped 'round the woods. First thing, they'd blow, and down came a bird. They killed squirrels and caught fish with their blow guns.

Some Africans hold to voodoo. Some put a dime in the shoe to keep bad spirits away. Some carry a buckeye in the pocket to keep off cramp and colic. A bone found in the jawbone of a hog, they say, make chillun teethe easy.

I believe in hants. I was going along one night by Denham fill and I heard a chain rattling along the crossties. Couldn't see a thing, but that chain just a-rattling clear as a bell. I heard tell, back since the war, a convict working on the railroad was killed by the boss, beat to death. And the cap'n threw the man's body in the fill. I couldn't see a thing, but that chain was a-rattling, right where that convict was buried. I believe the Lord took care of me that night and I hope He keeps on doing so.

WPA interviewer: Annie Lee Newton
Athens, Georgia

THE GHOSTS
WHOOF AND WHIFF

You want to hear 'bout ghosts, eh? Just ask
me, George Brown. I was a boy on Edisto Island. I lived at Vinegar Hill, next to Cassina
Point, the plantation home of Missus Carolina
de Lafayette Hopkinson. I saw plenty of ghosts
'round the plantations, like Peters Point, and
the rest of the island. They sure is worrisome
things. Ain't worry me so much lately 'cause I
done learned where they stay and I keep out of
their path. But last year, in this here same
month of January, it seemed like every turn I
made I saw a spirit, once the sun went down
good.

When I was a young boy, my granny told
me zackly what to do if you want to sperience a
ghost. She said I must take mucous out of a
dog's eye and place it in my eye. I tried that
plan one night just for deviltry. You know how
boykind is—always wants to try some new prank.

Well, as I said, I tried the plan out. My old
dog went by the name of Lion. I sneaked up to

Lion when he was 'sleep by the fire and stuck my finger in his eye. The dog let out a yell and jumped through the window. I saw his tail go 'round the corner. Good-bye, dog. After he was gone, I stuck the same finger that been in Lion's eye in my own eye, and I put on my cap and left the house.

Well, sir, I had scarce gone a hundred steps 'fore I saw something dancing 'fore my eyes like a swarm of big birds. I know they wasn't birds though, 'cause they had long legs and long arms like people. But they flew 'round just like buzzards. They started to whoof and whiff. Then I really got scared. I shut my eyes tight and ran. That night I reckon I knocked 'gainst 'bout every tree in the Big Woods, but I didn't care. Had to get away from them ghosts 'fore they took my mind away.

After that, I never took nothing out of a dog's eye and put in my eye. I done satisfied myself 'bout ghosts, brother. You liable to see ghosts anyhow in your traveling. It ain't no use to seek them out.

WPA interviewer: Chalmers S. Murray
Charleston, South Carolina

THREE WOMEN WITHOUT HEADS

My pappa's name was Handy Jones and my mammy's name was Melissa. She belonged to Marse Whitaker, but after she married, she belonged to Marse Rufus Jones. My name is Martha.

Marse Jones owned a sizable plantation near Cary, North Carolina. He was good to his slaves. Never whipped none of us. I heard a whole heap 'bout the patterollers from my mammy, but I don't remember that.

I remember 'specially when the Yankees came. Was on a Thursday and the old master was sick in bed. He had sent some slaves to the mill with grain. When them men started back from the mill, the Yankees overtook the wagon. They killed the oxes in the harness and cut off the quarters. Then they rode to the big house with that meat a-hanging all over the horses. They threw what they didn't want away—course they took the meal and the grain.

The old master had heard them Yankees

was coming, and he buried the silverware in a sandbar. But Lawdy, them Yankees found it just like it was on top of the ground. They stole everything they got their hands on, 'specially the meat from the smokehouse. They went down to the cellar and drank up Marse's brandy and got so drunk they had no sense a-tall. When they left, they carried my brother off with them, and nobody ever heard from him again. I heard said the president wasn't thought much of in them days.

Marse Jones died a few days after the surrender, and it appeared like he made a will what gave all his slaves a little piece of land. Somehow this Marse Whitaker, what my mammy belonged to before, had something to do with it. So he went to the courthouse in Raleigh to have the will broke up. Then he dropped dead, right there. Marse Jones and Marse Whitaker were buried the same day.

You asked me 'bout ghosts. I'll tell you. I saw three ghosts, and my mammy saw them too. We was close to the Ephues Church on the Durham highway. The ghosts was three women, dressed in white, and they had no heads. They rose up and flew over the wagon and drifted to the churchyard cemetery. That was the last time I saw them. I ain't believed in ghosts much till I saw them that night. But, Lawd, I saw them and I believe now.

WPA interviewer: T. Pat Matthews
Cary, North Carolina

THE GHOST STOLE
MY OVERCOAT

My name is George Brown. Vinegar Hill is my home, on Edisto Island, South Carolina. I've encountered all kinds of ghosts in my life, but there was one played a mean trick on me. It happened like this:

I attended a meeting one night at Old House. We had a nice time. Deacon August Mannery held forth and we all gave testimony. I can't say why hard luck tracks me! Maybe I ain't come out plain with my testimony. Anyhow, five minutes after I left Jonas Bright at the crossroads, a ghost butted me.

It was sharp cold and I had on my brand new overcoat my wife's cousin's child gave me. I knew full well that overcoat was going to hold me back. I started to run like crazy, but there was too much weight 'cross my shoulder. The ghost closed in on me. I jumped off the road and dodged behind a toothache tree. The ghost followed. I broke loose and made for Bear Hog Bottom, where the tall cypress trees grow. I figured I could hide somewhere in that swamp, 'cause ghosts don't like to cross water. Big mistake! The mud was awful deep, and I bogged down.

The ghost wasn't far behind. No time to tarry. I loosened my shoe and pulled one foot out, then the other. I got back on the road again. Thank the Lord.

I looked back and saw a big white thing, bigger than a cow, coming up fast. That thing could run! I knew if he could beat *me*, he was good all right, 'cause everybody knew I could run! I sped up. My tongue was hanging out till it 'most touched the ground. The ghost slipped up and grabbed me from the back, and I knew I was lost then sure enough.

But I was very nimble, so I slipped out of my overcoat right quick and jumped. I left the ghost holding that overcoat and got away from that place. I done got my second wind and I kept on running to Steamboat Landing Road and turned in at my brother's house.

I never saw my brand new overcoat again. I swear, I don't know what a ghost would want with an overcoat, 'cause they don't wear no clothes. Anyhow, he got it and he kept it. I ain't going to follow no ghost to hell for no overcoat. No, sir.

That just shows you how ghosts stand. They're so plaguish like. Torment the living spirit out of a man. That was the first ghost I ever met that had the thieving habit.

Interviewer: Chalmers S. Murray
Charleston, South Carolina

THE GHOST OF FENWICK HALL

I am George Brown of Edisto Island, but I know 'bout Johns Island. Fenwick Hall been a big plantation house on Johns Island. Marse Edward Fenwick, Jr., a Tory and lover of race horses, owned that big red-brick manor house. Marse Fenwick was so hated in the colonies his British friends furnished a guard for his house.

The ghost at Fenwick Hall shows right frequent. All the Fenwick descendants is said to be born with a caul over the face and they see that ghost—and hear the crying too. The Fenwicks have the gift, the power of second sight, and can see ghosts. The English writer, Amelia E. Barr, what wrote *The Bow of Orange Ribbon*, was one of them. She had some sort of magical sight.

One of Marse Fenwick's daughters, said to be the fairest of them all, got on one of her father's swiftest thoroughbred horses with a young man. They galloped away to elope. Word got to Marse Fenwick. He rounded up some men and they made chase on their horses. They overtook the daughter and the man at Stono Ferry.

Marse's daughter was jerked off the horse. The boy was kept on the horse's back. They had a mock court, right there under a big oak tree, and they convicted the boy as a horse thief. The girl wailed and cried out for them to stop. Her earnest pleas was not regarded.

Marse Fenwick produced a rope. A noose was tied and the loop pulled over the boy's head. Then the rope was tied to an oak limb. Marse Fenwick handed the girl his riding crop. He said, "Hit the horse on the hind quarter." She said, "No." He told her she must. He ranted and raved. He insisted, he said. When the girl hit the horse, it ran ahead and left the boy dancing in the breeze, his neck in the hangman's halter.

The girl watched the boy die, then went insane. Marse Fenwick assigned her to a room in the attic. Even after the poor girl's death, she ranted and raved and wailed in the garret.

All them Fenwicks what been born with a caul over their face hear that sound and see the ghost.

WPA interviewer: Chalmers S. Murray
Charleston, South Carolina

A FLOCK OF GHOSTS CAME JUMPING 'CROSS THE ROAD

I, George Brown, live on Edisto Island.

Been near four years since I saw a ghost or smelled a spirit. Back then, I was seeing a girl who lived on the far side of Zion Church. I went to see her one night and parted from her 'bout ten o'clock to head back to Vinegar Hill where I lived.

When I reached the public road, the half-moon shone down. I saw the path tolerably well and made good time till I got close to the church. I was trying to sashay past when a flock of ghosts came jumping 'cross the road. They came from the well where they was drinking water. Now they was ready to get back in the grave. I stopped and let them pass. I counted. Lord in Heaven! Five hundred spirits, moving fast with their feet in the element. Spirits never track the ground.

I ain't scarcely know what to do. One mind told me to run. 'Nother mind said, "Stay where

you be. Spirits ain't got you to study about." I
stood, trembling. Seemed like I shook the earth
'neath my feet.

Soon all the ghosts crossed on over and lit
down in the graveyard. They done reached
home. Once the spirits quenched their thirst, everything was all right.

Then I felt my feet move, and when I
came to myself I realized I was halfway to Vinegar Hill. I must have run all of five miles. I
slowed down to catch my breath and take a
chaw of tobacco. Then I lit out again. Soon I
was in my own house. My nerves was so weak
I slept for two whole days. You never going to
catch me 'round Zion Church again, not when
the moon is only half full.

WPA interviewer: Chalmers S. Murray
Charleston, South Carolina

GHOSTS IN BOTTLES

According to the interviewer, Sam Bailey claimed to know all about the habits of ghosts: their familiar haunts, their favorite trees, the time they leave the graveyard, and the way they smell— to name a few. He said ghosts have never been known to attack a human physically, but they can scare a person to death. Sam had a bad reputation among his neighbors. They distrusted him, believing he was in league with the powers of darkness. He was crippled and ugly as sin. He had a vicious temper and once bit off the tip of an opponent's tongue in a fight. Most of his neighbors feared him, but they respected his prowess. Anyone who could bottle ghosts, they declared, should be given a wide berth.

I'm Sam Bailey of Edisto Island, South Carolina. I know exactly how to deal with ghosts who make a nuisance of themselves 'round my premises. I bottle them. Ain't everybody who can do that. You got to study years and years for that skill. Things like that come with wrinkles and a white head.

Ghosts 'round my place kept me awake for nights on end till I learned to catch them in bottles. I spent hours preparing a charm I placed in the bottom of the bottle. I never told no one what made up the charm, except for one ingredient: chamber lye. After I stirred all together, it took a right smart time to set.

While the mix was setting, I heard the ghosts raising ruckus in the backyard. Their favorite stunt was to run up and down the clothesline. Then, they dropped to the ground with a loud thud. Annoying.

I didn't want no ghost to come in the house. I couldn't sleep then. It made me shudder to think about a ghost passing his cold hands over the soles of my feet.

After the charm set, I put the bottle under the clothesline. The charm was so powerful, ghosts couldn't help but fall in. I corked the bottle and put it under my bed. After I kept the ghosts in the bottle the entire night, them ghosts didn't bother me no more.

You ask me how ghosts smell. They smell like ghosts—that's all I can tell you. How you speck they smell?

WPA interviewer: Chalmers S. Murray
Charleston, South Carolina

THE WITCH'S TRIAL

I live near Lancaster, South Carolina. My mammy told me 'bout a young girl who claimed she knew a witch. The witch went by the name of Barbara Powers. She was an old woman from Chesterfield, South Carolina.

The girl testified that one evening she was weary from her task and lay down on the bed. Then the witch, Barbara Powers, dropped in and sat on top of her. The witch pressed her hands on the girl's throat and made her cough and choke. The girl couldn't get no breath and thought she was going to die. Instead of death, the witch turned the girl into a horse. She mounted the "horse" and off they trotted through the woods to the main part of Lancaster.

The girl said the witch went through the keyhole of several shops in the town. Time after time she came out of the keyhole with stolen goods and piled them on the horse's back. When the witch had loaded much as the horse's back would hold, she mounted and rode off to her home in Chesterfield. That was a hard trip for that poor horse.

The witch unloaded the booty. Then she mounted again. "Off to Cheraw," she said, whacking the horse on the side. The horse hotfoot it in that direction. The witch robbed stores in Cheraw in the same manner she stole goods in Lancaster. Finally, she rode back to her home in Chesterfield and unloaded that loot. Then she rode back to Lancaster and changed the horse to the girl again.

The girl said the witch's supernatural power did all that, and the hard ride ruined her health. Misery welcomed her every morning, she said, and the slightest toil taxed her beyond endurance. The girl had to go early to the fields when the dew was heavy on the cotton and she could hardly make it.

The girl told her fam'ly and friends all about the witch. The friends went to Chesterfield and brought the old woman by force to Lancaster. They made the woman touch the girl and say over her, "God bless you." Those certain words, they said, released the girl from the spell. They said the girl instantly recovered.

This whole thing made Barbara Powers mad as an old setting hen. She brought a lawsuit in the court against them certain persons laying hands on her and forcing her to go to that girl's house.

Judge David Johnson was the judge at that particular time, in 1813. You might know, he was later elected governor of South Carolina. Stephen D. Miller was one of the lawyers. He was governor number twenty-five.

The judge listened to all of them testify. When the girl finished her story, the judge said, "Stop." He listened to the girl's friends say they very gently brought the old witch from her home in Chesterfield. I tell you, ma'am, I wonder how gentle them men could have been working with a witch.

Anyhow, that judge didn't believe in such as witches. He just listened out of curiosity. That was the last court trial in America what allowed testimony about witchcraft. My mammy said she worried about that young girl after that day.

WPA interviewer: Genevieve Chandler
Murrells Inlet, South Carolina

Other sources that were consulted:
- "Touring Lancaster County With Grandfather," 1954, compiled by Viola Caston Floyd, for the Lancaster County Historical Commission.
- "Tours," 1956, Viola C. Floyd. Lancaster County Historical Commission, Lancaster, S. C.

THE WENCH
WAS A WITCH

I'm Richard Moring, eighty-six years old.
Marster Anderson Clemmons owned my
mammy, Cherry, and Marster Fielding Moring
owned my pappy, Jacob. I don't know much
about Marster Moring, 'cause we stayed with
Marster Clemmons, near Apex, North Carolina.

Marster Clemmons owned less than a
dozen slaves, but he was good to them. The
overseer, Mr. Upchurch, whupped them some.

We had enough to eat and wear, and we
worked hard. Marster allowed us our own garden and potato patch, and we had our own
hogs.

They allowed us some fun like dancing,
wrestling matches, swimming, fishing, hunting,
and games. We also had prayer meetings at our
cabins. When there was a wedding, there was
fun for all, 'cause it was a big affair. Everybody
got all dressed up in new clothes, and marster's
dining room was decorated with flowers for the
occasion. The band, which was banjo and

fiddle, played. All the neighboring folks came to the wedding.

I did hear tell of the supernatural, as you say. My grandmammy told me a story about the witch at the mill when I was a little fella. I'll tell you about it if you wants to hear.

There was a free slave what owned a mill, and he was making a heap of money. After he married a handsome wench, it appeared like his luck went bad. The folks quit bringing their corn to the mill to be ground, and he began to get poor. Word got around that the wench he married was a witch.

In them times, slaves who ran away from cruel marsters went to the mill and was give a place to sleep. Late one night a slave boy ran away. He boasted he wasn't scared of nothing. He had a butcher knife, he said, if need arose.

As the moon waned, the runaway saw something frightening, and the whites of his eyes shone like lamps. The thing came nearer and nearer, and the boy saw it was a big black cat with the savage notion of eating him. The runaway swung his knife and off came one of the old cat's feet. She gave an awful screech and jumped out the window.

The next morning the mill owner's wife was sick in bed and refused to get up. Her husband insisted she get up and cook his breakfast, but she refused to stir.

"You better get up, you lazy trollop," the man shouted. With that, he dragged the woman out of the bed. He was amazed when he saw her hand was cut off. He yelled for the neighbors.

After the runaway explained that a fiery cat attacked him during the night and he cut off the cat's paw, the neighbors made a big brush pile, then tied the witch on the top and burned her up.

After that, the mill owner's luck changed. He became prosperous and married a fine woman and lived happily all of his life.

WPA interviewer: Daisy Bailey Waitt
Raleigh, North Carolina

THE BLEAK HALL JACK-O'-LANTERN TANGLED ME UP

I go by the name of George Brown. I live on Edisto Island. I know about all them highfalutin' plantation homes, like Sea Cloud and Bleak Hall. Sea Cloud house was named for the families who built it, the Seabrooks and the McLeods. It was a spectacle, but nothing compared to Bleak Hall. Now that was a mansion for sure!

Bleak Hall woods got plenty of treasure hidden in them. All the treasure been hidden since Rebel Time. Rebel Time folks was tricky. They knew zackly where to store away their money and silver things and they fixed them so you couldn't get at them handy. Trouble is, they formed the plan so good it was mighty hard to locate their treasure.

Every living time them Bleak Hall people hid something in Bleak Hall woods, they set a Jack-o'-Lantern to watch over them. You know about Jack-o'-Lantern?

This is what you do when you got a treasure you want to keep secret. First, you dig a
deep hole in the woods near some kind of tree,
oak or pine. Then you go out and kill an animal and bury it with the money. The animal's
ghost will haunt the spot and guard the buried
hoard with their spirit. Some folks kill a setting
hen to guard the valuables. Other folks kill an
enemy and cut the head off and bury them with
the treasure. After that, when anybody comes
around, the Jack-o'-Lantern rises out the hole
and hovers over the treasure.

Jack-o'-Lantern is a light what shines in the
moonlight. Some folks call him "money lights."
Now I don't tell you what I don't know. I've
been through all of that, yes sir.

Only last March I hunted treasure in Bleak
Hall woods. Before I started out, I heard a
rattle in the woods. When a chain rattles in the
middle of the night deep down in the woods,
you can be sure the noise is made by a Jack-o-
Lantern rubbing himself against a tree.

Next night I made tracks for the woods.
Heavy fog settled down over the earth. Stars
scarcely showed through. Frogs hollered in the
tussock. It wasn't a very good night to be away

from home. I said to myself, "Suppose you find treasure. What a blessing that will be."

I turned off the public road and made tracks through the big woods. Nothing stirred. All the varmints was asleep. When the moon showed himself I was not far from the place where the chain rattled. When the tree came into sight, I left the road and circled 'round the tree. Got my shovel on my shoulder, ready to dig.

I circled 'round the tree, one time, two times, then I stopped and studied my mind. I figured if I walked straight and didn't see nothing, my path was clear. I could start to dig beneath the tree. So I led off. I hadn't gone three steps before the moon shone on a dog what rose right up out of the ground and ran shimble-shamble by my feet. Oh, the moon did shine! I saw the dog good. His back sagged way down like it was broke, and his ear was 'most chewed off. Had three legs in back instead of two. Jack-o'-Lantern, sure as I been born!

I retreated back to the road and waited a good ten minutes. The dog faded from sight. I started off again. This time a calf, with his hide peeled off till the blood dropped, crossed my path. Never since my mammy borned me have I seen a sight like that. Water dribbled out of my mouth. The hair rose taut on my head. All my sins came across my mind. Maybe God didn't mean for me to have that treasure after all.

I thought about all the need in my house and I made one more try. A light shone over the treasure. The Jack-o'-Lantern ran 'tween my legs and tangled me up and threw me right in the mud. My face was buried in the stinking mud. Seems like I was in that diametrical spot over four hours. Ants crawled over me, rats crawled over me, maybe snakes, I ain't able to say.

When I came to my senses, the moon had gone down and the stars was out bright. Jack-o'-Lantern was gone. The frog stepped up his noise and the crickets started to sing in the tree-tops. Way over yonder I heard a fowl crow. Here it was 'most dayclean and I was in the Bleak Hall woods with my face covered with dirt and my skin all grafted with vines, and not a thing to show for all the trouble. The treasure was still beneath the ground, and I was on top of the ground.

I went home with my head drooped low. Ain't breathed a word to no person, I was so ashamed.

Next time I'll know better. Jack-o'-Lantern ain't nothing to fool with. All they do is tangle you up. Make you forget where the treasure is buried.

WPA interviewer: Chalmers S. Murray
Charleston, South Carolina

THE BLACK RACER

My name is Di, and they call me the marster of the cookstove. I cooks for Marster Neyle on his plantation near Summerville and at his home in Charleston when he's in residence there. Marster had a big manor house, and my cabin was on the far side of the vegetable garden. The garden was enclosed with a white picket fence.

One morning, while Marster Neyle was reading on the piazza, I was coming along the picket fence when I saw a black racer cross my path. I vowed never to take that path again. No, nevermore. The black racer done trampled there, and I didn't want to tangle with him. That was his territory and I was going to leave it alone. The racer was the boss at that place. I made for home in a jiffy.

After the breakfast hour passed, Marster came to my cabin to see about me. I told him I could not cook for him ever again.

"But, why Di?" he asked.

"I'm sorry, suh," I said. "I'm sorry I got to give up my job, but that black devil ran over my path this morning, and I sure can't come to that house no more."

"What black devil?" asked my marster.

"The black racer. He trampled over that path, and that means I can't come to your house no more."

"Well, if you cannot come to my house, I'll just have to move my house to yours," he said. "You have to cook for us."

"No, suh, I can't never cook for you no more. I'm too sorry."

Marster tried to reason with me, but his spostulations was in vain.

"Di, I think I heard of that before," he said. "I heard tell that if you go back to the exact place where the racer crossed your path, make a cross on the ground, and walk backwards over it, you'll never be bothered by the black racer again."

I flew from my cabin, went to the tramping ground of the black racer, and carried out the instructions. It worked. I never saw the black racer again. I sure was glad to know about that charm. If I ever was to see another black racer, I'd do the same.

WPA interviewer: Jessie A. Butler
Charleston, South Carolina

THE DOGS
LOOKED SCARED

My mother was owned by Massa Zeke Long, and Pappy was owned by the same, but they did not live in the same house. I'm Will Dill and I lived with my mother. From my calculation, I was born about 1862.

You know what a jack-leg preacher is? When he marries a man and woman, he tells them, "Jump backwards and forwards over that broom. Now, you're man and wife." My mammy and pappy was married by a jack-leg preacher.

Massa's plantation was in Anderson County, not far from Three and Twenty Mile Creek. Massa asked me, "What the rooster say? What the cow say? What the pig say?" He got amusement out of my kiddish replies.

I was just a boy when one day I saw lots of wild turkeys in Massa's yard. I ran after the little wild things, but I never caught a one. The old mother hen flew from one limb in a tree to another limb in another tree and called to them. They was the runningest things I ever saw. I about ran myself to death but I never did get one.

I know a lot about fowl. I'll tell you something. They talk like we do. I often notice a rooster and hens standing 'round in the shade talking. The rooster says something and the hens listen, then answer him back. One day I heard a turkey hen say, "We are poor. We are poor." The old turkey gobbler said, "We can't help it. We can't help it." They talk, but taint everybody can understand them.

We had lots of animals 'round the plantation. Plenty of fowl. Hogs ran wild in them days. Now and then one of the men on the plantation would shoot a wild hog and we had plenty of meat to eat.

One night we boys was out with our dogs possum hunting, and the dogs treed a possum in a little scrubby tree. I was always a good climber, so I headed up the tree to shake the possum out. I shook and shook but the possum would not fall. I shook so hard my hat fell off and I told them boys not to let the dogs tear up my hat.

I couldn't figure out what was holding that

critter to that tree limb. I knew it wasn't a skunk 'cause we couldn't smell nothing. But when I looked again, that animal got bigger and bigger. I scrambled down the tree, nearly falling out of it. The dogs acted kind of scared, yet they ran up to the tree and barked. One old dog did not bark, he just hollered. I believe that thing in the tree might have been a ghost. Iffen it was a possum, it would have fell out when I shook the tree.

You ask about the war. When we heard them Yankees was coming, we took all Massa's good horses to the woods and hid them, leaving only two or three poor old nags in the stable. The Yankees came, but they left them poor horses. They only took good ones. They shucked Massa's corn and fed their horses. We stayed on at Massa's plantation for some time after 'mancipation.

WPA interviewer: F. S. DuPre
Spartanburg, South Carolina—District 4

GHOSTS ARE
GOOD COMPANY

I'm Solbert Butler, age of eighty-two. Back in slavery time, I lived on old Massa Ben Bostick's place in Hampton County, South Carolina. The plantation's been divided since them days, 'tween Ben Bostick, Iva Bostick, Joe Bostick, Luther Bostick, Eddie Bostick, and Jennie Jo Bostick.

I couldn't number the plantations old Massa Ben Bostick owned. He was a millinery. The house the family lived in they called the Paradise House. No one went to that house but only the rich. Oh, it was paradise at Christmas.

Old Massa was good to us. And he whipped us good too! Tied some to the fence post and whipped them. The overseer, Mr. Aldridge, was a mean man. The field hands got licked till the blood came out. Then red pepper and salt was rubbed on the back. My uncle was so whipped he went into the woods and lived there for many months. Had to learn the independent life.

Oh, my God! Can you say them as done such as Mr. Aldridge ain't going to their reward? Oh my God no! That man can't have no rest. He did the field hands so mean, finally old Massa heard about it. And when he heard about it, he discharged him.

Massa took me as a pet. Had a little bed right by his own and took care of me. Every morning, a house servant brought in his tray, and Massa fed me from it. Massa took me in the carriage with him. He kept two fine horses just for the carriage.

Ghosts? I'm used to them. I see them all the time. Good company! They come in my house. Sometime I walk along at night and see them. The big house was full of them. White folks see them too. That is, some white folks. One day I saw a white man walking to work up at the big house and I told him he ought to see the ghosts. The white man turned and ran away.

They is a sight! They play. They dance 'round and 'round. They're happy all right. But they devil you too. They don't scare me. They talk to me. If I meet them in the road, they pass the time of day with me.

"Morning, Solbert. How you feeling?" they say.

"Just so-so."

"Uh-huh."

They all look alike.

One ghost pushed me over in the ditch.
"What you do that for?" I said.

"That ain't nothing," he said.

I talk to them just the same as if they was somebody. Some folks outgrow them. But not me. You have to be born wrapped in the caul to see them. But if you ain't, you can't see them.

WPA interviewer: Phoebe Faucette
Scotia, South Carolina

THE THING WAS COMING RIGHT TO THE HOUSE

My name is Charlie Davis. I couldn't tell you how old I am, only as I ask Massa's son and he told me I was born ahead of him 'cause he had the day put down in the family book. I must be about eighty-eight. I belonged to Massa George Crawford's people. Massa George is the one what died up here one of them other years not far back. They was my white folks.

We chillun lived well and had plenty good ration to eat all the time 'cause my mammy cooked for the Missus there in the big house. All we chillun lived in a one-room house right there in the white folks' yard and ate in the Missus' big kitchen every day. They gave Mammy and she chillun just such things as the white folks ate, like biscuit and cake and ham and coffee and hom'ny and butter and all that kind of eating. Didn't have no need to worry about nothing a-tall. Massa had a heap of other colored peoples there besides we, but they never lived that way. There was about eighty of them.

I'll tell you about what I experienced. I saw them things what people call ghosts. One night I heard something and I looked out at the garden we had planted beside the road. A great big black thing was making right for the house. I called my mammy and said, "Look yonder." The thing was coming fast. Mammy hurried and lit up the lamp. I heard people say if you don't light up the lamp when you see a spirit, it will surely come in and run you out. I knew that big black thing was nothing else but a spirit. Nothing else.

WPA interviewer: Annie Ruth Davis
Marion, South Carolina

I MET MANY A GHOST

I am Isaiah Butler. Ain't much left of me now. I'm about seventy-nine years. I know all about this here country. I was born and raised right here on the Bostick place. Lived here all my life apart from traveling 'round a little space. There was a rice field not far from this house.

This place joined the Thomson place. And the Thomson place to the Edmund Martin place that was turned over to Joe Lawton, his son-in-law. Bill Daniel had charge of the rice field I was telling you about. He was overseer on the Daniel Blake place. Then there was the Maner place, the Trowell, the Kelly, and the Wallace places.

Way back they cultivated rice. Had mules to work it. But cotton and corn was what they planted most of all. Four thousand acres I think they tell me was on this place. S'posed to be more than ten miles square. When the Bostick boys came back from out west last year, they had to come to me to find out where their place is. They didn't know nothing about it.

Back in them old days twenty plows was
used, and the hoe hands numbered over a hundred. Cotton used to be hauled by ship to Savannah. That was a long way from Hampton
County, South Carolina. Wagons carried the
crop to Cohen Bluff, Matthews Bluff,
Parichucla. They hauled it right along this road.
Railroad changed all that, you know.

Old Massa Ben Bostick used to bring
clothes and shoes to us and saw that we was
well cared for. I was just a little boy, too young
to do nothing. Just played 'round in the street.
There was nineteen houses in the street for us
colored folks.

When the slaves did all their day work,
they would go home and cook their supper and
wash up. If somebody's day work hadn't been
done, they got put in the stocks or the bill-bo.
A horn blew at a certain time for slaves to go
to bed. Sometime they had to outen the fire
and finish their supper in the dark. The
underdriver, he would go 'round and see who
hadn't gone to bed. He wouldn't say nothing
then, but next morning he reported to the overseer. Them as hadn't gone to bed got whipped.

There wasn't no jails in them times. Them

as done wrong, they whipped them and they sold them. Every slave knew what "I'll put you in my pocket, sir!" meant.

Saturday was a work day but not Sunday. Rations was given out on Monday.

Edmund Lawton went over to Louisiana to work on the Catherine Goride place, but he came back, 'cause he said they blew their horn for work on Sunday same as any other day, and he said he wasn't going to work on no Sunday.

I remember when the Yankees came through. I was 'bout ten years old. Massa had a big gin house, barn, stable, and such like. And when the soldiers came, a goat was up on the platform in front the door to the barn loft. There was some steps leading up there and that goat walked up them steps same as anybody. The first thing the Yankees did was shoot that goat. Then they tore up everything. All the white folks had taken refuge up North, and the Yankees didn't do nothing to the slaves.

I've met plenty of ghosts. One got me in the water once. And another time, when I was crossing a stream, I was on the butt end of the log, and a ghost was on the blossom end, and we met just as close as you and me is now. I said to the ghost, same as to anybody, "I sure ain't going to turn back and fall off this log. Now, best thing for you to do is turn 'round and let me come after you." It don't pay to be 'fraid of them. So he wheeled 'round—spirits can wheel, you know. And when he got to the end of the log, I said, "Now you off and I'm off. You can go 'cross now."

Ghosts sure is a thing, all right. They look just like anybody else, 'cept cloudy and misty like it's going to pour down rain. White folks see them too, you know. I don't see them no more. Must have outgrown them.

WPA interviewer: Phoebe Faucette
Hampton County, South Carolina

THE GHOST REVEALED BURIED TREASURE

My name is Janie Gallman, and I am eighty-four years old. My mammy, my pappy, and me belonged to Marse Bill Keenan in Union County, South Carolina. His place was situated 'tween the Pacolet River and Fairforest Creek, near where Governor Gist had a plantation.

I played with the chillun of the white overseer. We jumpd rope most of the time. When the overseer left home to spend the night somewheres else, they sent for me to spend the night with the family. They was poor white trash.

Mammy and Pappy had a nice garden, and I ate my share of the vegetables out of that garden. I saw plenty wild turkey 'round the place, but I never saw no hogs and cows run wild. Massa Keenan was a good man. I never saw no slave in chains nor whipped. After 'mancipation, Massa gave each slave a barrel of meal, a wagon of corn, and a cow and a half.

One night a woman ghost came to our neighbor's cabin and she just sat on the front steps and said nothing. Several nights in succession she did the same. One night my neighbor's husband asked the ghost what did she want, and why she sat on the steps and said nothing. The ghost spoke then and told him to follow her. He followed and she led him to the basement of their house and told him to dig in the corner. He did just that. Pretty soon, he unearthed a jar of money. The woman ghost told the man to take a certain amount for himself and give the rest to a particular person. The ghost told the man if he didn't give the money to the person she named, she would come back and tear him apart. He obeyed, took the amount she said and gave the rest where the ghost directed. After that, the woman ghost never came back again.

WPA interviewer: F. S. DuPre
Spartanburg, South Carolina

THE BALLOON
SPIT OUT A
STREAK OF FIRE

My name is Amos Gadsden, not Gadson,
like some call it. I was born on St. Philip's
Street in Charleston, South Carolina. That's
where old Miss lived then. We belonged to
Marse Titus Bissell. I don't rightly know the
year I was born, but I was nineteen years old
when the war started. Missus had my birth written down in the family Bible, but that was lost
in the war.

My grandmother was a daily gift to the old
Missus when they was chillun. Grandmother
was Affy Calvert and she was trained up in the
service of her missus. She was nurse to all the
chillun and grandchillun. She lived to be over a
hundred years and died at the Bissell home on
Rutledge Avenue years and years after slavery.
My mammy, Ellen, was a laundress and my father was coachman. He also tended the yard.

I never did get a slap from my Missus. If
she corrected me on something, I nearbout

cried. Sometime I slept at the foot of Missus' bed. It ain't every little boy got to do that.

We spent the summers in Charleston and winters on Cypress Plantation, near Green Pond. The smokehouse was always filled with meat, and the fields and gardens gave plenty to eat. There was some bad people on the plantation. You can make yourself respectable, but some never do.

I was trained by old Tony for yard work. I looked out that no harm came to the older chillun, but one day they got away from me. They went to play on the logs at the lumber yard. The water was filled with timber, open to the Ashley River, and the tide was running out.

One of the boys got on a log, and two others on another log, and the little scamps began to paddle. But when they found themselves in the tide—oh, Lord—they screamed at the top of their voices. I wasn't far off and heard them. I jumped in the water and swam to get a bateau. When they saw me, they hushed up. The tide had carried them some distance before I caught up with them, down near Chisholm Rice Mill. Marse Chisholm saw the whole thing and gave me a five-dollar Confederate bill for saving the chillun.

One evening, early dusk, in the winter, I was with two white boys on the corner of Hasell Street and East Bay. We stopped to watch a balloon floating slow in the sky. I never saw nothing like it before. It was a pretty site. While we was looking, a streak of fire came straight down from the balloon to Russell's Planing Mill at the foot of Hasell Street, next to us. Right quick the mill caught on fire. Nothing could put it out. One building after another caught fire. Big flames jumped from one place to another.

The first church that burned was the Circular Church on Meeting Street. Then Broad Street and the Roman Catholic Church, and St. Andrews Hall, what was right next to the Roman Catholic Cathedral on Broad Street. That balloon flew on down to Beaufort, I heard tell.

Yes, ma'am, I saw it drop that fire on Russell Mill. To this day, I think about that balloon spitting that streak of fire. I never saw nothing like it before or since.

During the war, I went to Virginia with Dr. H. E. Bissell, in the Army. He was a surgeon. A camp of slaves went ahead to prepare the roads—pioneers, they was called. I remember Captain Colcock. Honey Hill—terrible fighting.

Fight and fight. Had to platoon it. I was behind the fighting with Dr. Bissell. I held arms and legs while he cut them off. Hard times came to the Army. Only corn to eat.

When the bombardment came to Charleston, the family moved to Greenville. I was still in Virginia with Dr. Bissell. The railroad bridge across the Ashley River was burned to prevent the Yankees from coming into Charleston. The ferryboat *Fannie* crossed the river to make connections with the Savannah Railroad. Them Yankees was destroying railroads as they came down. Sherman set fire everywhere he went— didn't do much fighting, just destroying.

WPA interviewer: Martha S. Pinckney
Charleston, South Carolina

GLOSSARY

ancestors — forefathers; family members who lived
   and died before you were born
apprehend — take into custody
ascend — go upward
astride — with a leg on each side
attic — a room directly under the roof
bateau — flat-bottomed row boat
bed (the fire) — stoke or tend the fire
belly — swell with wind, as a ship's sail
bittle — food
blues — despondency
bog — to sink down, as in mud
boisterous — loud
bolt — a movable rod that fastens a door
boneset — a North American plant, also called
   thoroughwort
booty — loot or plunder taken by robbery
brogans — heavy leather shoes
buckeye — the nutlike seed of a horse chestnut tree
buckra — white people
butcher knife — a large knife used for cutting big
   pieces of raw meat
butt — hit with the head
buzzard — a broad-winged, soaring hawk
cargo — freight of a ship
carte blanche — whatever you please; complete
   freedom of choice
cassino — a game of cards in which the ten of
   diamonds counts two points and the two of

spades counts one, with eleven points constitut-
ing the game
castor oil — medicine made from castor bean
caul — membrane
chimley — chimney
chullun — children
chunk — throw
circulation — the flow of blood in veins
conjure — to call upon a spirit for a spell
consecrated — dedicated to the service of the Deity
cooter — turtle
cork — a bottle stopper made of cork
crave — to long for
creepy — unearthly
crop — a riding horse whip
crossties — timber laid in cross direction on a
    railroad track
cutaway — morning coat, long in back
dayclean — dawn
devilment — abuse, harassment
deviltry — mischievous behavior
diametrical — direct; absolute
diminish — reduce
dispute — argument
doctrine — principle; position
drench — to wet thoroughly
drove — a group
dumplings — small balls of dough boiled in broth
eerie — creepy; supernatural
element — the earth; the ground
elongated — extended

elope — run away to get married
empower — enable
entangle — ensnarl; intertwine
expostulate — reason earnestly with a person
feat — accomplishment
fill — a hole in the earth where trash is thrown
firefly — lightning bug
frivolity — an act that is not serious
frolic — fun
frugal — thrifty
fuss — excessively busy with trifles
gay blades — dashing young men
ghastly — horrible
girdle — woman's undergarment used for support
gourd — a large fruit whose dried shell is used as
    a container or a dipper
graft — a plant in a groove or slit
grease — lard; rendered fat of hogs
grip — hold
groom — one responsible for the care of horses
grotesque — unnatural; misshapen and ugly
gully — a ditch or ravine
halter — a noose
hand — help, as in a helping hand
hatch — deck opening, as on a ship
heist — hoist, lift up
hideous — gruesome
highfalutin' — of high society
hinge — a jointed device on which a door swings
hoard — to store away money or valuables in
    large quantities

hogshead — a cask containing from 63 to 140
  gallons
hominy — ground corn
hypnotic — having the ability to charm or hypnotize
in the element — above the ground
inroads — foray; encroachment
inveigle — entice; ensnare
jib — triangular sail set forward
jiffy — a short time
ketch — catch
lam — hit; strike
lard — rendered fat of a hog
Leonid — a meteor shower
liable — likely
list — lean to one side
locust — grasshoppers
loft — room under a sloping roof
'low — allow
'lowed — allowed
magnitude — great amount or size
'mancipation — emancipation, freedom
massacre — barbarous warfare
meditation — contemplation
millinery — millionaire; one who is worth at least
  a million dollars financially
moccasin — a snake; water moccasin
monk — a man who is a member of a religious
  order
mullet — fish
nag — an unhealthy horse
nimble — graceful in movement

noose — a loop with a running knot

nuisance — annoyance

opponent — person on opposing side in a contest

oppressed — troubled with a heavy burden

ox — a bovine or cow

pallet — a bed or mattress of straw

partake — to take a part or share in something

particle — a very small bit

passel — a group or lot of undetermined number

peculious — peculiar; odd

perzackly — exactly

pester — annoy

phantom — an apparition or specter

physic — medicine

piazza — porch

pillar — a column, as on a house; upright structure supporting a porch roof or entryway

pine knot — a joint in a pine limb, rich in resin

plague — epidemic disease

plait — braid

plank — wooden board

platoon — a military unit

plumb — absolutely; completely

poke — a burlap bag that holds cotton

port side — left side of a vessel, looking forward

prance — move by springing

precedent — a preceding case that serves as an
example

precipice — overhanging a vertical cliff or face

predecessors — ancestors

prehensile — able to grasp things, as of an
   animal's foot or tail
premises — a specified tract of land with buildings
   on it
prey — victim
prowl — plunder; rove about
pummel — beat or thrash
quench — satisfy
racer — a snake of the genera Coluber and
   Masticophis
racket — noise
ractified — wrecked; destroyed
recoil — shrink back
regatta — sailboat race
reprimand — punish verbally; fuss at
restraint — restriction
rheumatism — a medical condition causing pain
   and stiffness
right smart — a large amount
rioters — people who cause great disturbance
ritual — an established procedure
rowdy — rough; disorderly
sacred — holy
sashay — move nonchalantly
sass — talk back to
scheech — fearsome; terrifying
scrubby — with very little foliage
scruples — acts of restraint; morals
sea horse — a fish of the pipefish family having a
   long snout

seining — to catch fish with a large net
seven-up — a card game
shinplaster — paper money of a denomination
   lower than a dollar
skeptical — having doubt
slant — slope
snout — nose
Sooky — name of a cow on his plantation
speck — expect
spectacle — impressive kind
sperience — experience
s'pose — suppose
spostulated — expostulated
squat — crouch low to the ground; sit on one's
   bent legs
squinch owl — screech owl
stagecoach — covered horse-drawn passenger
   carriage used as public transportation
steelyard — a portable weighing device
sulfur — a yellow nonmetallic element
supernatural — outside what is explainable by
   natural laws
swarm — a great number of things in motion
symbol — emblem; token
tackle block — used with ropes for hoisting
tarriance — delay; sojourn
tarry — linger
task — a designated piece of work
taut — tightly drawn
tax — a burden
tear-down — a loud, rowdy meeting

tedious — long and tiresome
teethe — growing teeth
tentative — hesitant
thicket — a dense growth of bushes
toil — hard work
tonic — liquid medicine
tradition — custom
tread — walk
treed — forced an animal to take refuge in a tree
tremor — involuntary shaking
trollop — an untidy woman; a woman of loose
  morals
turpentine — pine tree resin
tussock — clump of grass
twas — it was
twix — between
uncanny — weird
upshot — the final issue
varmint — creature; animal
vexation — annoyance; irritation
vibration — a quivering or trembling motion
vow — a promise; a pledge
wane — decline in strength or power
waver — sway
wench — a good-looking young woman
wheel — to turn around, as if on an axis
whiff — a slight outburst
willy-nilly — unwillingly; helplessly; by compulsion
wrestle — engage in struggle for mastery
zackly — exactly
zistence — existence

NANCY RHYNE is a storyteller and much-sought-after speaker with a keen interest in southern folklore. Nancy lives with her husband Sid in Myrtle Beach, South Carolina.

Contact Nancy through:

SANDLAPPER PUBLISHING CO., INC.
PO BOX 730
ORANGEBURG, SC 29116
1-800-849-7263

Nancy Rhyne's books are available through local bookstores, libraries, and directly from Sandlapper.

John Henry Rutledge
The Ghost of Hampton Plantation

Using the voice of Sue Alston, a daughter of emanci-
pated slaves, Rhyne relates events that took place on
Hampton Plantation in South Carolina over the course
of a couple centuries. Based on interviews with Sue
Alston, who died in 1983 at the age of 110.

Paperback
BW photographs
112 pages
ISBN 0-87844-131-X

Coastal Ghosts

A guide to sites of ghostly appearances and mysterious happenings along the coast, from Wilmington, North Carolina, through South Carolina's fabled Low Country, to Savannah, Georgia.

Paperback
BW photographs
192 pages
ISBN 0-87844-049-6

Plantation Tales

Nancy Rhyne introduces the reader to the age of peacocks, palaces, and Charleston balls through a selection of tales. Covers the strip of coast stretching from Wilmington, North Carolina, to Savannah, Georgia.

Paperback
BW photographs
162 pages
ISBN 0-87844-093-3

Southern Recipes & Legends

Both Nancy Rhyne and her husband Sid are terrific cooks. This volume of favorite Rhyne family recipes are flavored with tales of Charleston, Beaufort, and Savannah.

268 pages

Hardcover
ISBN 0-87844-133-6

Paperback
ISBN 0-87844-134-4